THE ULTIMATE SCHOLARSHIP BOOK WORKBOOK

PLANNING SHEETS, BUDGET TRACKERS
& APPLICATION TIMELINES

LIYA MONROE

GRAPEVINE BOOKS

Published by

GRAPEVINE BOOKS

www.grapevinebooks.com

email: contact@grapevinebooks.com

Ordering Information:

Quantity sales: Special discounts are available on quantity purchases by corporations, associations, and others.

For details, reach out to the publisher.

First published by Grapevine Books, 2026

CONTENTS

Section 1

Scholarship Readiness & Goal Setting

Scholarship Mindset & Motivation

When it comes to securing scholarships, your mindset and motivation play pivotal roles. **Developing a strong scholarship mindset** is the first step in successfully navigating the application process. A positive and determined attitude can propel you forward when the journey gets tough, especially during challenging times or when dealing with setbacks.

To cultivate a scholarship mindset, start by reframing how you view the application process. Rather than focusing on the hurdles or competition, view scholarships as an opportunity for growth. Think of each scholarship application as a stepping stone that not only brings you closer to your educational goals but also strengthens your resilience and perseverance. Remember, each essay you write, every document you submit, and every recommendation you request is not just a task; it's part of your growth as a student and individual.

Motivation is the engine that drives your mindset. Without motivation, it's easy to feel overwhelmed by the process. Scholarship applications require time, energy, and effort. One way to maintain motivation is to remind yourself of why you're applying in the first place. What are your long-term educational goals? How will these scholarships help you achieve them? Whether you're looking to attend a prestigious university, reduce financial stress, or focus on your studies without the burden of debt, your goals should serve as constant reminders of the reward waiting for you.

Set both **short-term and long-term goals**. Short-term goals might include completing one application per week, drafting essays on specific days, or reaching out for letters of recommendation by a certain date. These bite-sized objectives will help break the process into manageable chunks, making it less daunting. Long-term goals should focus on securing the scholarships necessary to achieve your ultimate educational and career aspirations.

Another crucial element of motivation is **self-belief**. You must believe that you are worthy of the scholarship opportunities you are applying for. Self-doubt can be a significant barrier, but remember that scholarships are designed to support students who show potential, commitment, and passion for their chosen field. If you put in the effort, your chances of success increase. Scholarship committees are looking for well-rounded individuals who have both academic ability and a drive to succeed.

You should also **surround yourself with supportive individuals**. Sharing your goals with family, friends, or mentors can help keep you accountable. Not only can they offer valuable advice and guidance, but they can also remind you of your worth when you begin to lose sight of it. The scholarship journey is rarely smooth, but having a support system can make it easier to navigate.

Lastly, **celebrate small victories** along the way. Each completed scholarship application is progress. Whether it's submitting your first essay or meeting a scholarship deadline, these milestones will boost your confidence and keep your motivation levels high.

In conclusion, developing a scholarship mindset requires a focus on growth, belief in your abilities, and a strong sense of purpose. By setting clear goals, maintaining motivation, and staying positive, you can increase your chances of success and achieve your educational dreams.

Defining Your Education Goals

Defining clear and achievable education goals is one of the most important steps in your academic journey, especially when applying for scholarships. Scholarships are competitive, and having a clear educational vision helps you target the right opportunities and present yourself as a committed, focused candidate. When you define your educational goals, you create a blueprint for your future that guides your decisions, applications, and efforts.

The first step in defining your education goals is identifying what you want to achieve in the **short term** and **long term**. Short-term goals are immediate objectives, such as completing your degree on time or maintaining a certain GPA. Long-term goals might involve pursuing a specific career, furthering your education with a graduate degree, or becoming an expert in a particular field. Having both types of goals is crucial because short-term goals keep you on track, while long-term goals provide direction and purpose.

Start with your passions and interests. Think about what excites you—whether it's solving complex problems, helping others, creating art, or working with technology. These passions often guide you toward a specific field of study. Reflect on the subjects you're most interested in and consider what career opportunities align with these interests. Are you passionate about health care, technology, environmental science, or business? Knowing what you want to study will help you define your educational path.

Next, consider the **level of education you want to pursue**. Are you aiming for a bachelor's degree, or do you plan to attend graduate or professional school? For instance, if you're interested in becoming a doctor, your educational path will likely include undergraduate studies followed by medical school. If you want to become a software engineer, you might focus on a computer science degree with plans to specialize further in graduate school. By identifying the level of education you want, you can better align your scholarship applications with your future aspirations.

Once you've decided on your field of study, it's time to set **specific, measurable, and achievable goals**. For example, a short-term goal could be to maintain a GPA of 3.8 or higher to be eligible for scholarships that require a minimum GPA. A long-term goal might be to graduate with honors or secure a job in your chosen field within six months of graduation. Make sure your goals are specific and actionable—

vague goals like "do well in school" won't be as effective as measurable goals like "achieve a 90% in all courses related to my major."

A key part of setting your education goals is breaking them down into smaller, manageable steps. For example, if your long-term goal is to attend graduate school, your short-term goals might include researching programs, securing recommendation letters, and preparing for standardized tests like the GRE. These steps will guide your actions and ensure that you're continuously moving forward in the right direction.

Finally, **review your goals regularly**. Life changes, and so may your goals. It's important to reassess your goals periodically and adjust them as needed. For example, you might discover a new interest in a field you hadn't considered before or decide that a different educational path is a better fit for your career aspirations.

Defining your education goals allows you to stay focused and intentional with your academic pursuits. It helps you prioritize tasks, apply for scholarships that align with your objectives, and ensure that your efforts are leading you to the future you envision. By setting clear educational goals, you're not just working towards a degree; you're building a foundation for lifelong success.

Personal Strengths Inventory Template

This template is designed to help **you track your personal strengths and skills**. You'll list your strengths, provide a description or example of each, evaluate how important each strength is to your **career goals**, and create an **action plan for improvement**. This will help you assess areas of growth and track your progress toward strengthening these skills.

Category	Strength/ Skill	Description/ Example	Importance to Career Goals	Action Plan for Improvement
Academic Skills				
Leadership				
Communication				
Creative Thinking				
Time Management				
Teamwork				
Adaptability				

Academic Snapshot Worksheet Template

This worksheet allows **you to monitor your academic progress** by tracking important academic data such as your **GPA**, **test scores**, and **extracurricular activities**. It helps you set targets, evaluate your current standing, and plan the necessary actions to achieve your academic goals.

Category	Details	Current Score	Target/ Goal	Action Plan
GPA (Grade Point Average)	Cumulative GPA			
SAT/ACT Scores	SAT Score			
Advanced Placement (AP)	AP Subject 1 Score			
	AP Subject 2 Score			
Class Rank	Current Class Rank			
Extra-Curricular Activities	Activity 1 (e.g., Sports, Debate, etc.)			
	Activity 2 (e.g., Volunteering, Leadership)			
Awards & Achievements	Award 1			
	Award 2			
Standardized Tests (if applicable)	Other tests (e.g., GRE, Subject Tests)			

Extracurricular & Leadership Tracker Template

This tracker allows **you to log your extracurricular activities and leadership roles**, making it easy to see how you've developed leadership skills, teamwork abilities, and more. You can track the **position/role** you held, the **dates** you were involved, and the **skills** you developed from each activity.

Activity/Role	Position/Role	Dates Involved	Skills Developed & Impact
Club/Organization 1			
Club/Organization 2			
Sport 1 (e.g., Soccer)			
Sport 2 (e.g., Tennis)			
Volunteer Leadership			
Student Government			
Academic Clubs			
Artistic Pursuits			
Cultural Clubs			
Other Extracurricular			

Activity/Role	Position/Role	Dates Involved	Skills Developed & Impact
Special Projects			
Leadership Experience			

Volunteer & Community Service Log Template

This log helps **you track your volunteer and community service hours**, while also reflecting on the **skills and impact** you've gained from each activity. It's a great way to record your involvement in important community work and demonstrate the value of service in your personal growth.

Service/Project	Organization/ Location	Hours Volunteered	Impact & Skills Gained
Project 1			
Project 2			
Fundraising/Charity Event			
Community Clean-Up			
Tutoring/Mentorship			
Volunteer Work at Events			
Soup Kitchen/Feeding			
Hospital/Health Center			
Animal Shelter			
Environmental Causes			
Cultural/Religious Events			
Other Volunteering			

Awards & Achievements Record Template

This template is for **recording any awards, honors, or recognitions** you've received. By listing each **award**, **organization**, and **date received**, you can reflect on the significance of each recognition and highlight these accomplishments in your scholarship applications or resume.

Award/Honor	Awarding Organization/ Institution	Date Received	Description & Significance
Award/Honor 1			
Award/Honor 2			
Award/Honor 3			

Award/Honor	Awarding Organization/ Institution	Date Received	Description & Significance
Academic Achievement			
Athletic Recognition			
Volunteer/ Community Award			
Leadership Award			
Creative Achievement			
Service Award			
Special Program/ Certificate			
Scholarships or Grants			
Other Recognitions			

Skills & Talents Brainstorm Template

This spreadsheet is designed to help **you list and categorize** your skills and talents. It lets you track **proficiency levels** and understand how each skill can be applied in your academic and personal life. Use this to focus on areas that align with your **career or scholarship goals**.

Skill/Talent	Category	Current Proficiency Level	Application/ Use
1	Academic		
2	Leadership		
3	Communication		
4	Creative/Artistic		
5	Technical/IT		
6	Problem-Solving		
7	Organizational/Time Mgmt		
8	Collaboration/Teamwork		
9	Research/Analysis		
10	Public Speaking/Oral		

Skill/Talent	Category	Current Proficiency Level	Application/ Use
11	Foreign Languages		
12	Other		

Long-Term Scholarship Goals Template

This template is designed to help you track your long-term scholarship aspirations. You can list your specific goals (for example, "Win a scholarship for graduate school"), identify the target scholarships (such as particular scholarship programs), define a timeframe for achieving these goals (like the next two years), and outline the action steps you need to take (for example, improving your GPA or applying to specific scholarships). You can also track your status and make additional notes about your progress to stay on course..

Goal	Target Scholarship(s)	Timeframe	Action Steps	Status/Notes
Goal 1				
Goal 2				
Goal 3				
Goal 4				
Goal 5				
Goal 6				
Goal 7				
Goal 8				
Goal 9				
Goal 10				

Short-Term Scholarship Targets Template

This template is for breaking down **short-term, actionable steps** that you can take to achieve scholarships in a smaller timeframe (like within a semester or year). You can define **specific scholarship targets** (such as "Apply for three local scholarships"), list the **deadlines** for each target (like application due dates), outline **action steps** (such as drafting essays or gathering recommendation letters), and track your **status** and make **notes** to ensure you're staying on track with deadlines and requirements.

Target	Target Scholarship(s)	Deadline	Action Steps	Status/Notes
Target 1				
Target 2				
Target 3				
Target 4				

Target	Target Scholarship(s)	Deadline	Action Steps	Status/Notes
Target 5				
Target 6				
Target 7				
Target 8				
Target 9				
Target 10				

Section 2

Scholarship Research & Organization

Scholarships are a critical resource for many students seeking higher education, and understanding the different types of scholarships available is essential for maximizing your opportunities. There are several categories of scholarships, each with its own criteria, purpose, and eligibility requirements. In this section, we'll explore the various types of scholarships and what makes each one unique. By understanding these categories, you can tailor your scholarship search and application strategies to fit your needs and goals.

1. Merit-Based Scholarships

Merit-based scholarships are awarded to students based on their academic achievements, talents, or other personal merits. These scholarships do not consider financial need but instead recognize a student's dedication, hard work, and potential for success in their studies.

Merit-based scholarships are some of the most sought-after awards because they offer significant financial support and often have higher award amounts. These scholarships may be awarded by colleges, universities, government agencies, and private organizations. Criteria for eligibility typically include GPA (Grade Point Average), standardized test scores (such as the SAT or ACT), extracurricular activities, leadership qualities, and even artistic or athletic abilities.

To apply for merit-based scholarships, you'll typically need to provide transcripts, test scores, and an essay or personal statement that demonstrates your strengths and achievements. Some merit-based scholarships are renewable for multiple years, meaning if you continue to meet the academic requirements, you can receive the scholarship for the entire duration of your degree program.

2. Need-Based Scholarships

Need-based scholarships are awarded to students who demonstrate financial need. These scholarships are designed to make education more accessible for students who might not be able to afford the cost of tuition, fees, and other college expenses without additional financial support.

Need-based scholarships are typically awarded by government agencies, private organizations, and colleges or universities themselves. The eligibility for these scholarships is usually determined by a family's financial situation, and students are often required to submit documents like the Free Application for Federal Student Aid (FAFSA), tax returns, or other proof of income.

The amount of the award can vary depending on the student's financial need, which is calculated using a formula that considers household income, assets, family size, and other factors. Need-based scholarships are essential for many students, as they provide the financial relief necessary to attend college without the burden of excessive student loans. Unlike merit-based scholarships, which focus on academic performance, need-based scholarships emphasize the financial situation of the student and their family.

3. Athletic Scholarships

Athletic scholarships are awarded to students who excel in sports and plan to participate in intercollegiate athletics at the college level. These scholarships are offered by colleges and universities with athletic programs and are often tied to specific sports, such as football, basketball, track and field, soccer, and swimming.

To be eligible for an athletic scholarship, students must demonstrate exceptional athletic ability and potential in their chosen sport. Many schools have recruiters who scout high school athletes to offer them athletic scholarships. In some cases, students may need to attend tryouts or provide video footage of their athletic performance as part of the application process.

Athletic scholarships can be partial or full awards, meaning they may cover only part of tuition or all expenses, including tuition, room and board, and even books. These scholarships can be highly competitive, as the athletic department at each college or university may only have a limited number of scholarships available each year. In exchange for the scholarship, student-athletes are expected to compete for their school's sports team and maintain certain academic standards.

4. Minority Scholarships

Minority scholarships are specifically designed to support students from underrepresented groups, including ethnic minorities, racial minorities, and gender minorities. These scholarships aim to encourage diversity in higher education by providing opportunities for students who have historically been underrepresented in college and university settings.

The eligibility criteria for minority scholarships vary depending on the specific scholarship and its intended demographic. These scholarships can be based on ethnicity, race, sexual orientation, or even disability. For example, there are scholarships specifically for African American, Hispanic, Asian, or Native American students, as well as those for women in certain fields like engineering or technology.

Minority scholarships can be offered by government agencies, private organizations, corporations, and colleges and are often intended to promote greater access to education and to encourage diversity in academic disciplines where specific groups may be underrepresented.

5. Private Scholarships

Private scholarships are awarded by organizations, businesses, foundations, and non-profits that are not affiliated with specific colleges or universities. These scholarships can be based on a variety of factors, including academic achievement, financial need, community service, or specific personal qualities. Private scholarships may be open to students from all backgrounds or may be targeted toward specific groups, such as first-generation college students, women in STEM, or students with disabilities.

Private scholarships often have less stringent eligibility requirements than merit-based or need-based scholarships, and the application process may be less competitive as well. However, there are thousands of private scholarships available, and many students can benefit from applying to a wide range of these opportunities. Some private scholarships require essays, letters of recommendation, or even personal interviews as part of the application process.

6. Employer-Sponsored Scholarships

Some employers offer scholarships to their employees or the children of employees as a benefit or incentive. These scholarships may be based on merit, financial need, or other criteria determined by the employer. Employer-sponsored scholarships are often renewable, meaning students can receive financial support for multiple years as long as they meet the required criteria.

These scholarships can be a great way to offset the costs of education, and many large corporations or businesses offer these opportunities. For example, some companies provide scholarships to the children of employees, while others may offer scholarships for employees pursuing higher education or further career development. To apply for these scholarships, students or their parents will typically need to contact the company's human resources department for more information about the available programs and eligibility requirements.

7. Research/Essay Competitions

Some scholarships are awarded through essay contests or research competitions. These scholarships are awarded to students who submit the best-written essays on a specific topic or research project. The competition may be related to academic subjects, social issues, or creative writing.

These scholarships encourage students to engage in critical thinking, research, and creative expression while providing an opportunity to showcase their skills. The essay or research competition may be hosted by nonprofit organizations, corporations, or professional associations. In most cases, students will need to follow strict guidelines, such as word count or topic scope, and may be required to submit their work by a specified deadline.

8. Government Scholarships

Government scholarships are awarded by national, state, or local governments to help students afford higher education. Federal scholarships, such as those administered by the U.S. Department of Education, include programs like the Pell Grant and the Federal Supplemental Educational Opportunity Grant (FSEOG). These scholarships are typically need-based, and eligibility is determined by your FAFSA (Free Application for Federal Student Aid).

State governments also offer a variety of scholarships and grants for residents attending in-state colleges or universities. These state-funded scholarships may be need-based or merit-based, and the eligibility requirements and award amounts vary by state. Students should check with their state's education department or state grant agency for available opportunities.

Understanding the different types of scholarships is essential for maximizing your chances of receiving financial aid for your education. By knowing the specific requirements and eligibility criteria for each scholarship, you can tailor your applications to match the scholarship's goals and increase your chances of success. Whether you are applying for merit-based, need-based, or private scholarships, there is a wide variety of opportunities available, and with the right mindset and strategy, you can find the financial support needed to pursue your academic and career goals.

Scholarship Eligibility Comparison Sheet Template

his template helps you compare the **eligibility criteria** for multiple scholarships at once. You can fill in the **scholarship names**, the **specific eligibility requirements** (e.g., minimum GPA, field of study, community involvement), and the **required documents** (e.g., transcript, essay, recommendation letters). The **deadline** column helps you track the submission date for each scholarship, ensuring you stay organized and on top of deadlines.

Scholarship Name	Eligibility Criteria	Required Documents	Deadline/Date
Scholarship 1			
Scholarship 2			
Scholarship 3			
Scholarship 4			
Scholarship 5			
Scholarship 6			
Scholarship 7			
Scholarship 8			
Scholarship 9			
Scholarship 10			

Essay Requirement Tracker Template

This template is for **tracking the essay requirements** for each scholarship application. For each scholarship, you'll list the **essay prompt or topic** and the **word count requirement** (to make sure your essay is within the required length). The **deadline/date** column helps you ensure that you meet the submission deadlines for each scholarship essay.

Scholarship Name	Essay Prompt/Topic	Word Count Requirement	Deadline/Date
Scholarship 1			
Scholarship 2			
Scholarship 3			
Scholarship 4			
Scholarship 5			
Scholarship 6			
Scholarship 7			
Scholarship 8			
Scholarship 9			
Scholarship 10			

Recommendation Letter Requirements Template

This template helps you manage the **recommendation letter requirements** for each scholarship. You'll list the **type of recommender** required (e.g., teacher, employer, mentor) and any specific **requirements for the letter** (e.g., format, content, submission process). The **deadline/date** column ensures that you submit your recommendation letters on time and gives you a place to keep track of who has written the letter for you.

Scholarship Name	Recommender Type	Requirements for Letter	Deadline/Date
Scholarship 1			
Scholarship 2			
Scholarship 3			
Scholarship 4			
Scholarship 5			
Scholarship 6			
Scholarship 7			
Scholarship 8			
Scholarship 9			

Scholarship Name	Recommender Type	Requirements for Letter	Deadline/Date
Scholarship 10			

Scholarship Requirement Checklist Template

This checklist allows you to list each scholarship along with its **eligibility criteria** and **required documents**. You can use the **"Completed/Notes"** column to mark whether you've gathered the necessary documents or completed each requirement. This will help you keep track of the status of your scholarship applications and ensure you don't miss any critical components.

Name	Eligibility Criteria	Required Documents	Completed/Notes
1			
2			
3			
4			
5			
6			
7			
8			
9			
10			

GPA & Transcript Tracking Template

This template helps you **track the GPA** and **transcript requirements** for each scholarship application. In the **Required GPA** column, you will note the GPA requirement for the scholarship. The **Current GPA** column allows you to track your academic standing and determine if you meet the eligibility criteria for each scholarship. The **Transcript Submitted** column is where you can indicate whether or not you have submitted your official transcript for each scholarship (marked as "Yes" or "No").

Scholarship Name	Required GPA	Current GPA	Transcript Submitted
1			Yes/No
2			Yes/No
3			Yes/No
4			Yes/No
5			Yes/No

Scholarship Name	Required GPA	Current GPA	Transcript Submitted
6			Yes/No
7			Yes/No
8			Yes/No
9			Yes/No
10			Yes/No

Scholarship Notes & Research Pages Template

This template provides a space for **important notes** about each scholarship, such as specific eligibility criteria, tips, or deadlines that you need to remember. The **Scholarship Website** column allows you to keep track of the online application portals or sources for further research. This will help you stay organized and ensure that you have all the information needed to apply successfully.

Scholarship Name	Eligibility Criteria	Important Notes	Website
1			
2			
3			
4			
5			
6			
7			
8			
9			
10			

Scholarship Contact Information Log Template

This template is designed to help you **track important contact information** for each scholarship organization or institution. In the **Scholarship Name** column, list the scholarships you're applying for. The **Contact Name** and **Organization/ Institution** columns provide space to write down the primary contact person's name and the name of the organization or institution offering the scholarship. Lastly, the **Contact Email/Phone** column ensures you have the correct contact details for follow-up communication.

Scholarship Name	Contact Name	Organization/ Institution	Contact Email/ Phone
1			
2			
3			
4			
5			
6			
7			
8			
9			
10			

Scholarship Follow-Up Tracker Template

This template helps you **track follow-up actions** for each scholarship. After you submit your application or if you have questions, it's important to follow up with the scholarship provider. The **Follow-Up Date** column allows you to note when you plan to check in or follow up. In the **Method of Contact** column, you can specify whether you reached out via **email**, **phone**, or **other methods**. Finally, the **Outcome/Response** column is where you can record the result of your follow-up, such as receiving a confirmation or additional instructions.

Scholarship Name	Follow-Up Date	Method of Contact	Outcome/Response
1		Email/Phone/Other	
2		Email/Phone/Other	
3		Email/Phone/Other	
4		Email/Phone/Other	
5		Email/Phone/Other	
6		Email/Phone/Other	
7		Email/Phone/Other	
8		Email/Phone/Other	
9		Email/Phone/Other	
10		Email/Phone/Other	

Section 3

Application Planning & Timelines

Monthly Scholarship Calendar Template

The **Monthly Scholarship Calendar** template is a powerful tool for organizing and tracking your scholarship applications. It allows you to visualize and manage important **deadlines** for each scholarship across the entire year. By listing the scholarships you're applying for each month, you can ensure that you don't miss any crucial dates. This template also provides space for **tasks and notes** related to each scholarship, such as **gathering documents**, **writing essays**, or reaching out for **recommendation letters**. By breaking down the application process month by month, you can approach your scholarship applications in an organized and manageable way. With this calendar, you'll have a clear overview of what needs to be done each month, helping you stay on track and avoid last-minute rushes. It's especially helpful for keeping track of multiple applications with varying deadlines, ensuring you never miss an opportunity.

Month	Scholarship Name	Application Deadline	Tasks/Notes
January			
February			
March			
April			
May			
June			
July			
August			
September			
October			
November			
December			

Weekly Application Planner Template

The **Weekly Application Planner** template is designed to break down your scholarship tasks into **smaller, weekly chunks**, helping you stay organized and focused on meeting deadlines. This planner gives you a clear overview of the specific tasks that need to be completed each week, such as **writing essays**, gathering **recommendation letters**, or submitting **application forms**. With this weekly breakdown, you can allocate enough time for each task, ensuring that no detail is overlooked. You'll also be able to see which scholarships require immediate attention and prioritize tasks accordingly. The **deadline column** ensures that you stay on track, keeping you aware of upcoming dates and helping you manage your time efficiently. This template is ideal for maintaining consistent progress on your scholarship applications, preventing procrastination, and ensuring that each task is completed on time. It's a helpful resource for students aiming to stay organized and reduce the stress of last-minute submissions.

Week	Scholarship Name	Tasks/To-Do	Deadline
Week 1			
Week 2			
Week 3			
Week 4			

Rejected Scholarship Reflection Template

The **Rejected Scholarship Reflection** template helps you **analyze reasons for rejection** and improve future applications.

1. **Scholarship Name**: Record the scholarship's name for reference.
2. **Reason for Rejection**: Reflect on why your application was rejected. Consider feedback or areas where you might have fallen short, like eligibility, competition, or missing documents.
3. **Lessons Learned**: Think about what you can improve. Did you miss key elements? Did your essay align with the scholarship's goals? This step helps you identify areas for growth.
4. **Action Plan for Future Applications**: Use the lessons learned to create a strategy for future applications. This might involve **improving essays, securing stronger recommendations**, **ensuring eligibility**, or **applying earlier**.

Scholarship Name	Reason for Rejection	Lessons Learned	Action Plan for Future Applications
1			
2			
3			
4			
5			
6			
7			
8			
9			
10			

Daily Task Breakdown Sheets Template

The **Daily Task Breakdown Sheets** template is designed to help you manage your scholarship application tasks on a **day-to-day basis**. With this sheet, you can list all the specific tasks you need to complete for your scholarship applications, breaking them down into **small, manageable actions** that can be accomplished within a single day. This approach helps you **stay focused** and **organized**, ensuring that no task is left behind. For example, you might need to work on drafting an essay, gathering specific documents, or following up on a recommendation letter request. By detailing these actions daily, you can avoid feeling overwhelmed by the larger process and ensure consistent progress toward completing your applications. The sheet also allows you to track **progress** by checking off completed tasks, giving you a sense of achievement and motivation. This template is particularly useful for staying on track and managing multiple applications at once, helping you maintain productivity and meet deadlines.

Date	Task Description	Time Allocation	Status/Notes

Date	Task Description	Time Allocation	Status/Notes

Priority Ranking Worksheet Template

The **Priority Ranking Worksheet** template helps you **prioritize** the scholarships you are applying for based on various factors, such as **deadlines**, **award amounts**, **eligibility**, and the **effort required** to complete the application. With this worksheet, you can **rank each scholarship** in order of importance, allowing you to focus your efforts on the most valuable and time-sensitive opportunities first. This approach helps you avoid spreading yourself too thin and ensures that you are dedicating the right amount of time to the most impactful scholarships. By assigning each scholarship a priority level (high, medium, or low), you can effectively manage your time and avoid missing any important deadlines. This worksheet is especially helpful when you are juggling multiple applications, as it helps you maintain focus on what matters most and allocate your time and energy efficiently. It's a great tool for staying organized, reducing stress, and maximizing your chances of success.

Scholarship Name	Deadline	Award Amount	Effort Required	Priority (1-3)
1				
2				
3				
4				
5				
6				
7				
8				
9				
10				

Application Progress Tracker Explanation

The **Application Progress Tracker** is an essential tool for **monitoring the status** of your scholarship applications. This template helps you keep track of the **tasks** you've completed and those that still need attention for each scholarship. It allows you to break down the application process into **manageable steps** such as **writing essays, gathering recommendation letters**, or **submitting supporting documents**. By filling in the tracker, you can stay organized and ensure you don't miss any important steps along the way. Each application can be listed with its status (e.g., not started, in progress, completed) to give you a clear picture of where you stand. This tracking method helps you prioritize tasks, especially when you're dealing with multiple applications. Regularly updating your progress ensures that you stay on top of deadlines and have enough time to **make revisions** or **seek assistance** where needed. With this tool, you'll maintain focus and reduce the stress of managing several scholarship applications at once.

Scholarship Name	Task/Action	Status (Not Started/ In Progress/Completed)	Due Date	Notes
1				
2				
3				
4				
5				
6				
7				
8				
9				
10				

Multi-Scholarship Timeline Explanation

The **Multi-Scholarship Timeline** is designed to help you visualize and **organize multiple scholarship application deadlines**. This tool allows you to **map out deadlines** for various scholarships you're applying for, ensuring that you stay on top of each application's **submission date**. By clearly defining the **tasks** associated with each scholarship (such as **writing essays**, **requesting recommendation letters**, and **submitting documents**), you can avoid confusion and ensure everything is completed on time. The timeline provides a clear, **visual representation** of all your scholarship deadlines, making it easier to plan your schedule and manage your time. This tool is ideal for those applying to several scholarships at once, as it ensures that you won't miss any critical deadlines. Additionally, it helps you identify any overlap or potential conflicts in deadlines, so you can adjust your schedule accordingly. With this timeline, you can stay organized and **efficiently manage** your scholarship applications, giving you a higher chance of success.

Scholarship Name	Deadline	Task/Action	Date to Complete	Status/Notes
1				
2				
3				
4				
5				
6				
7				

Scholarship Name	Deadline	Task/Action	Date to Complete	Status/Notes
8				
9				
10				

Essay Draft Timeline Explanation

The **Essay Draft Timeline** is a crucial tool for **organizing and managing the process** of writing your scholarship essays. Scholarships often require multiple drafts and revisions to ensure that your essays are well-polished and effectively showcase your strengths. This timeline allows you to **break down the essay writing process** into manageable stages, ensuring that each draft is completed on time and that you have enough time for revisions. With this template, you can **set specific deadlines** for completing each draft, whether it's the initial outline, the first draft, or the final version. By outlining these stages in advance, you can avoid rushing through the writing process and ensure that your essay is as strong as possible. Additionally, the timeline helps you **prioritize** tasks, especially if you're applying to multiple scholarships with different essay prompts. Regularly tracking your progress will keep you focused and motivated to complete each draft in time for submission, giving you the best chance of success in securing the scholarship.

Scholarship Name	Essay Draft Stage	Due Date	Status/Notes
1	First Draft		
2	First Draft		
3	First Draft		
4	First Draft		
5	First Draft		
6	Second Draft		
7	Second Draft		
8	Second Draft		
9	Final Draft		
10	Final Draft		

Recommendation Request Timeline Explanation

The **Recommendation Request Timeline** is an essential tool for managing the process of securing recommendation letters for your scholarship applications. It's common for scholarships to require **letters of recommendation**, and these letters often come from teachers, mentors, employers, or other influential figures in your life. Since it takes time for your recommenders to write and submit these letters, it's crucial to **plan ahead**. This timeline helps you **track the deadlines** for each recommendation letter request, ensuring you reach out to your recommenders well in advance. It also provides space to record any specific **requirements** for the letters, such as particular qualities to highlight or submission instructions. By setting clear **due dates** and following up at appropriate intervals, you can ensure that your recommenders have enough time to write thoughtful letters and that you meet the scholarship deadlines without rushing. This timeline helps you stay organized and ensures that you submit all required documents on time, increasing your chances of securing the scholarship.

Name	Recommender	Request Sent Date	Deadline for Letter	Follow-Up Date	Status/ Notes
1					
2					
3					
4					
5					
6					
7					

Transcript & Document Timeline Explanation

The **Transcript & Document Timeline** is a tool designed to help you **track all the important documents** required for your scholarship applications. Many scholarships require supporting documents, such as **transcripts, proof of eligibility**, **financial statements**, or even **proof of extracurricular activities**. Missing or late documents can cause delays in your application process, so it's essential to stay organized. This timeline allows you to **list the required documents**, note **submission dates**, and track when each document is due. It also helps you stay on top of tasks like requesting official transcripts or gathering any additional paperwork. By keeping all required documents organized, you can avoid last-minute rushes and ensure everything is ready for submission before the deadlines. The timeline is especially helpful when managing multiple scholarship applications with different document requirements, helping you keep track of each scholarship's specific needs and ensuring you never miss a crucial submission.

Name	Required Document	Request Sent Date	Submission Deadline	Status/ Notes
1	Official Transcript			
2	Financial Aid Forms			
3	Recommendation Letters			
4	High School Transcript			
5	Proof of Extracurriculars			
6	Test Scores			
7	Other Supporting Documents			

Submission Confirmation Log Explanation

The **Submission Confirmation Log** is an essential tool for tracking the **status of your scholarship applications**. It helps ensure that all your materials, including essays, recommendation letters, transcripts, and any other required documents, have been **submitted successfully**. This log allows you to record the **date of submission**, the **method** of submission (e.g., online portal, email, mail), and the **confirmation status** for each scholarship. For example, you can note whether you received an **email confirmation** or if there's a **tracking number** to ensure your materials were delivered. Keeping track of submissions in this way helps you **stay organized** and provides a record of your efforts, so you can follow up with scholarship providers if necessary. This log is especially useful when you're applying to multiple scholarships, as it ensures that no applications are overlooked and that you've met all deadlines.

Name	Date of Submission	Submission Method	Confirmation Status	Notes
1			Yes/No/Not Received	

Name	Date of Submission	Submission Method	Confirmation Status	Notes
2			Yes/No/Not Received	
3			Yes/No/Not Received	
4			Yes/No/Not Received	
5			Yes/No/Not Received	
6			Yes/No/Not Received	
7			Yes/No/Not Received	

Missed Deadline Review Explanation

The **Missed Deadline Review** is designed to help you **reflect on missed scholarship deadlines** and identify ways to improve your time management for future applications. Missing a deadline can be discouraging, but it's important to learn from the experience to avoid repeating the same mistakes. This review allows you to list the **scholarship name**, the **missed deadline**, and the **reason for missing it** (e.g., lack of preparation, unforeseen circumstances, or poor time management). By reflecting on the cause, you can create an **action plan** to improve your organization and workflow moving forward. It's also helpful to note any **lessons learned** and **strategies** to implement in the future to stay on track, such as setting reminders, starting applications earlier, or using organizational tools like calendars or task lists. This process not only helps you avoid future mistakes but also turns setbacks into valuable learning experiences.

Name	Missed Deadline	Reason for Missed Deadline	Action Plan for Future	Lessons Learned
1				
2				
3				
4				

Name	Missed Deadline	Reason for Missed Deadline	Action Plan for Future	Lessons Learned
5				
6				
7				

Time Management Reflection Explanation

The **Time Management Reflection** template is designed to help you **evaluate** how effectively you manage your time during the scholarship application process. Time management is a crucial skill when juggling multiple applications, essays, and deadlines. This reflection allows you to assess whether you're dedicating enough time to your applications, if you're using your time wisely, and how well you're balancing other responsibilities. You can reflect on areas such as whether you've been starting your tasks early enough, if you've allowed ample time for research and revisions, and if distractions or procrastination have impacted your progress. By analyzing your time management, you can identify areas for improvement and create an actionable plan to stay on track. This reflection also gives you the opportunity to adjust your approach for future applications, helping you become more efficient and organized moving forward. Regularly reviewing your time management helps you develop better habits and ensures you're consistently meeting deadlines without stress.

Did I start my tasks early enough?

Response:

Improvement Plan:

Did I allocate enough time for research and writing?

Response:

Improvement Plan:

Was I distracted during work sessions?

Response:

Improvement Plan:

Was I able to stick to a schedule?

Response:

Improvement Plan:

How did I prioritize tasks?

Response:

Improvement Plan:

What can I do to improve my time management?

Response:

Improvement Plan:

Was I able to balance applications with other responsibilities?

Response:

Improvement Plan:

Stress & Burnout Check-In Explanation

The **Stress & Burnout Check-In** template is a vital tool for **monitoring your well-being** throughout the scholarship application process. Applying for scholarships can be a long and challenging journey, and it's easy to become overwhelmed. This check-in allows you to assess your **stress levels** and determine if you're experiencing symptoms of **burnout**, such as feeling fatigued, anxious, or unmotivated. You'll be able to track your **emotional state**, the **triggers** causing stress, and whether you're practicing self-care. Identifying signs of stress early helps you take proactive steps to manage it, whether through **relaxation techniques**, **taking breaks**, or adjusting your workload. This check-in is essential for keeping your mental and emotional health in check, preventing burnout, and ensuring that you can complete your scholarship applications without sacrificing your well-being.

Stress Indicator	Current Stress Level (1-10)	Possible Causes of Stress	Action Plan
Physical Fatigue			
Mental Fatigue			
Feelings of Overwhelm			
Difficulty Staying Focused			

Stress Indicator	Current Stress Level (1-10)	Possible Causes of Stress	Action Plan
Anxiety About Deadlines			
Lack of Motivation			
Burnout Symptoms **(e.g., irritability, lack of enthusiasm)**			
General Emotional State			
Steps Taken for Self-Care (e.g., breaks, relaxation)			

Productivity Reset Worksheet Explanation

The **Productivity Reset Worksheet** is designed to help you **regain focus** and **re-energize** when you feel stuck or overwhelmed in the scholarship application process. It's common to experience **burnout**, distractions, or a loss of motivation when managing multiple tasks, and this worksheet provides a structured way to **refocus** your efforts. The worksheet encourages you to assess where you are in the process, what's been hindering your progress, and how you can take proactive steps to get back on track. By **breaking down large tasks** into smaller, more manageable ones, you can make progress without feeling overwhelmed. It also prompts you to identify **priorities** and set **new goals** for the immediate future. This reset process helps you regain momentum, boost your productivity, and refocus on your scholarship applications with renewed clarity and energy. It's a useful tool when you feel you need to hit the reset button and take control of your time and energy again.

Task/Action	Current Status	Challenges/ Obstacles	Action Steps to Reset
Task 1			
Task 2			
Task 3			

Task/Action	Current Status	Challenges/ Obstacles	Action Steps to Reset
Task 4			
Task 5			
Break Down Larger Tasks			
Reorganize Priorities			
New Short-Term Goals			
Steps for Increased Focus			

Accountability Partner Notes Explanation

The **Accountability Partner Notes** template is a tool for keeping track of the **support** and **progress updates** from your accountability partner. An accountability partner is someone who helps keep you on track with your goals, offers encouragement, and holds you accountable for meeting deadlines. This template allows you to record the **dates** and **discussion points** from your regular check-ins, providing a space to note any feedback or **encouragement** you receive. You can use the notes section to track **goals** set during the meetings, **action items**, and **adjustments** you've made based on the partner's advice. This tool ensures that you stay focused and motivated by regularly reviewing your progress with someone who can help you stay committed. The Accountability Partner Notes sheet can serve as a record of your journey, helping you see how much you've accomplished and what areas need attention as you continue through your scholarship applications.

Check-In Date	Partner Discussion Points	Feedback	Next Steps
1			

Check-In Date	Partner Discussion Points	Feedback	Next Steps
2			
3			
4			
5			
6			

Summer Scholarship Plan Explanation

The **Summer Scholarship Plan** template is designed to help you **maximize your scholarship opportunities** during the summer months. Summer is an ideal time to focus on scholarship applications because you may have more **free time** to dedicate to the process, especially if you're not taking classes. This plan allows you to **outline specific goals** for the summer, including applying for scholarships, researching new opportunities, or preparing application materials such as essays and recommendation letters. You can use the plan to identify **target scholarships**, set deadlines for completing application materials, and track progress. This structure helps you stay on track and ensures that you don't miss out on scholarships that may have summer deadlines or early fall deadlines. By proactively planning your scholarship efforts during the summer, you can reduce stress during the school year and give yourself a better chance at receiving financial aid for the upcoming semester or year.

Name	Research Tasks	Application Deadline	Completion Date
1			
2			
3			
4			
5			
6			
7			

Gap Year Scholarship Planning Explanation

The **Gap Year Scholarship Planning** template is intended for students who are taking a **gap year** before continuing their education. A gap year offers time to explore different interests, gain work experience, volunteer, or travel, but it can also be an opportunity to apply for scholarships that specifically cater to gap year students. This template helps you **identify scholarships** that are available for students who are taking a break from their studies. You can also **track deadlines**, required documents, and any specific **eligibility requirements** for gap year scholarships. Additionally, the template allows you to plan how you'll use your gap year productively, whether that's through internships, volunteer work, or personal development. By organizing your scholarship applications for a gap year, you ensure that you're still working toward your educational goals while making the most of your time off.

Name	Eligibility Requirements	Documents Needed	Deadline	Application Status
1				
2				

Name	Eligibility Requirements	Documents Needed	Deadline	Application Status
3				
4				
5				
6				
7				
8				
9				

Section 4

Budgeting, Financial Aid & Money Tracking

Tuition Comparison Sheet Explanation

The **Tuition Comparison Sheet** is designed to help you **compare the costs of tuition** across multiple colleges or universities, making it easier to make an informed decision when selecting the best school for your needs. Since tuition is often the largest expense when attending college, this tool is invaluable for **budgeting** and planning your finances. This template allows you to list the **tuition rates** for each institution you're considering, along with any **additional fees** such as lab fees, registration costs, or student activity fees. You can also track **scholarships**, **grants**, or **financial aid** awarded by each school, and subtract those amounts from the total cost to understand your **net tuition**. This helps you compare the **out-of-pocket costs** more accurately. The sheet can also include columns to track **payment plans**, **due dates**, and **institutional policies** on financial aid renewal. By organizing the tuition costs in one place, you can make more confident and informed choices about which institution offers the best value for your education.

			Net Tuition	Total Tuition Cost	
Name	Deadline for Payment	Payment Plan Options	Scholarships/Grants	Additional Fees	Tuition Rate
1					
2					
3					
4					
5					

Housing Cost Tracker Explanation

The **Housing Cost Tracker** template is designed to help you track and compare the **housing costs** associated with attending different colleges or universities. **Room and board** are significant expenses for many students, and it's important to consider whether on-campus or off-campus housing is the most affordable option. This template allows you to list and compare **room and board** costs for each school, including the **type of accommodation** (e.g., dormitory, shared apartment, single room). You can also track any additional housing-related expenses, such as **utilities**, **internet fees**, or **meal plans**. The tracker enables you to calculate the **total cost of housing** for each semester or year, which can help you make a more accurate financial comparison when considering different schools. Additionally, you can add columns for **payment deadlines**, **deposit requirements**, or **refund policies** for housing, which will help you manage your payments and understand the financial responsibilities associated with each housing option. This tool ensures that you account for all housing-related expenses when planning for college, giving you a clearer picture of your total cost of attendance.

College/ University	Room Type	Room & Board Cost	Additional Housing Costs	Total Housing Cost	Deposit Required	Payment Deadline	Refund Policy
1							
2							
3							
4							
5							

Books & Supplies Budget Template Explanation

The **Books & Supplies Budget Template** is designed to help you track and compare the **costs** associated with books and other essential supplies for your education. By organizing the **school names** in the top row and placing the **categories** (such as **Books & Supplies Cost**, **Additional Fees**, **Total Cost**, etc.) in the leftmost column, you can easily compare these costs across different institutions. This layout allows you to **see a clear breakdown** of each school's costs, along with any **additional fees** that might be incurred. The final column, labeled **Name**, is where you can record details related to **payment plans** and the **deadline for payment**, ensuring you have all the necessary financial information to make an informed decision about where to attend. By tracking this information, you can efficiently plan your **financial responsibilities** and ensure that you're budgeting appropriately for books and supplies at each school.

Name	Books & Supplies Cost	Additional Fees	Total Cost	Payment Plan	Options	Deadline for Payment
1						
2						
3						
4						
5						

Transportation Budget Template Explanation

The **Transportation Budget Template** helps you manage and compare the **costs** associated with transportation to and from various schools. Similar to the Books & Supplies template, the **school names** are placed in the **top row**, while the **categories** (including **Transportation Cost**, **Additional Fees**, **Total Cost**, and **Payment Plan Options**) are listed in the **left column**. This allows for an easy side-by-side comparison of the transportation costs at each institution, giving you a clearer view of your total expenses. Additionally, you can track any **extra costs** related to commuting, such as **parking fees** or **public transportation** expenses. The **Payment Plan Options** and **Deadline for Payment** columns in the far-right allow you to assess the available **payment flexibility** and due dates for transportation fees, helping you plan your budget accordingly. By using this template, you can ensure that all transportation-related expenses are accounted for, so you can make an informed financial decision.

Name	**Transportation Cost**	**Additional Fees**	**Total Cost**	**Payment Plan Options**	**Deadline for Payment**
School 1					
School 2					
School 3					
School 4					
School 5					

Meal Plan & Food Budget Template

Name	Meal Plan Cost	Additional Food Expenses	Total Food Cost	Meal Plan Options	Payment Plan Options	Deadline for Payment
School 1						
School 2						
School 3						
School 4						
School 5						

Meal Plan & Food Budget Explanation

The **Meal Plan & Food Budget Template** is a tool designed to help you track and compare the **costs associated with meal plans** and **food-related expenses** at different institutions. By organizing the **school names** in the top row and listing important categories (such as **Meal Plan Cost**, **Additional Food Expenses**, **Meal Plan Options**, and **Payment Plan Options**) in the leftmost column, you can easily compare how much each school will charge for meals. This template allows you to break down the costs into specific categories, helping you account for **meal plans**, **extra food expenses**, and **payment options**. The **Deadline for Payment** column ensures that you're aware of any deadlines associated with meal plan payments, which is crucial for planning your finances. By using this budget, you can **compare meal plans** across schools and make sure that you're selecting a school that fits both your budget and food preferences.

Name of School	School 1	School 2	School 3	School 4	School 5
Meal Plan Cost					
Additional Food Expenses					
Total Food Cost					
Meal Plan Options					
Payment Plan Options					
Deadline for Payment					

Personal Expenses Budget Explanation

The **Personal Expenses Budget Template** is designed to help you track **additional personal costs** while attending school, including **clothing**, **health expenses**, **entertainment**, and other **miscellaneous costs**. Similar to the **Meal Plan & Food Budget**, the school names are listed in the top row, while the **personal expense categories** are placed in the leftmost column for easy comparison. You can break down your **personal expenses** into specific categories, helping you manage how much you'll need for **everyday costs**. The categories include essential costs like **health insurance**, **clothing**, and **entertainment**, as well as other personal expenses that may arise. By listing **payment plan options** and **deadlines**, you can stay on top of when payments are due for these expenses and any available **flexibility** in how they're paid. This budgeting tool ensures that you **account for all personal costs**, allowing you to plan your finances more effectively and make educated decisions about your college expenses.

Name	School 1	School 2	School 3	School 4	School 5
Personal Expenses Cost					

Name	School 1	School 2	School 3	School 4	School 5
Clothing/ Shopping					
Health/ Insurance					
Entertainment					
Other Personal Costs					
Payment Plan Options					
Deadline for Payment					

Total College Cost Calculator:

The **Total College Cost Calculator** template allows you to calculate the **total cost of attending each school**. It breaks down major expenses, including **tuition**, **room and board**, **books and supplies**, **transportation**, **personal expenses**, and any other costs that might apply. By adding up the costs for each school, you can get a clear picture of your **total financial commitment** and help determine which school fits best within your budget.

Name	School 1	School 2	School 3	School 4	School 5
Scholarship Name					
Award Amount					
Scholarship Type					
Deadline					
Required Documents					
Status (Awarded/Not Awarded)					
Notes					

Scholarship Award Tracker:

The **Scholarship Award Tracker** is a tool for keeping track of the **scholarships** you've applied for and the **amounts** you've been awarded. It helps you monitor **important dates**, including **deadlines** and required **documents**, and track the **status** of each scholarship (whether awarded or not). This tracker allows you to stay organized and ensures you're aware of any important follow-up actions you need to take, such as submitting additional materials or confirming the award. By keeping this information organized, you'll have a better understanding of how much financial support you have for your education.

Name	School 1	School 2	School 3	School 4	School 5
Scholarship Name					
Award Amount					
Scholarship Type					
Deadline					
Required Documents					
Status (Awarded/Not Awarded)					
Notes					

Grant & Aid Tracker Explanation

The **Grant & Aid Tracker** is designed to help you **organize and track** the various **grants** and **financial aid** opportunities you receive or apply for. As you explore funding options for your education, you may qualify for **grants** based on **need**, **merit**, or specific **programs**. This tracker allows you to record essential details such as the **grant name**, **amount awarded**, **eligibility requirements**, and **application deadlines**. It also includes sections to track the **status** of each application, so you know whether you've been awarded the grant or if you need to follow up. Keeping track of this information ensures you don't miss any important deadlines or lose track of your awarded grants. By organizing your financial aid in this way, you can clearly see how much you've been awarded and what still needs to be done for other opportunities.

Grant/Aid Name	Amount Awarded	Eligibility Requirements	Application Deadline	Status	Notes
Grant 1					
Grant 2					
Grant 3					
Aid 1					
Aid 2					

Student Loan Comparison Explanation

The **Student Loan Comparison** template is a tool for comparing various **student loan options** available to you. Understanding your **loan terms**, such as **interest rates**, **loan amounts**, and **repayment options**, is essential when considering taking on student debt. This template helps you break down the details of each loan, including **lender information**, **interest rates**, **repayment terms**, and **loan fees**. By tracking these details across multiple loans, you can easily compare your options and make an informed decision about which loans align with your financial situation and long-term goals. The comparison also includes fields to track whether the loan is **federal or private** and what **repayment plans** are available. Understanding these key details helps you evaluate which loan is the best fit for your education and repayment abilities.

Lender	Loan Type (Federal/ Private)	Loan Amount	Interest Rate	Repay-ment Terms	Fees	Repay-ment Options	Loan Status
Lender 1							
Lender 2							
Lender 3							
Lender 4							
Lender 5							

Debt Awareness Worksheet Explanation

The **Debt Awareness Worksheet** is an essential tool for understanding and managing any **student debt** you may incur during your college years. This worksheet helps you track **loan amounts**, **interest rates**, **repayment plans**, and the **total debt** you owe. It encourages you to review all **loan details**, ensuring you are fully aware of your financial obligations. You will also assess your **current debt levels** and estimate the **total cost** of your loans over time. By tracking this information, you can plan ahead for your **loan repayment** and gain a better understanding of your **financial future** after graduation. This worksheet helps you evaluate the **impact of debt** on your long-term financial goals and can provide insights on how to **manage** or **reduce** debt responsibly.

Loan Type	Loan Amount	Interest Rate	Repay-ment Plan	Monthly Payment Estimate	Total Re-payment Amount	Loan Start Date	Status
Loan 1							
Loan 2							
Loan 3							
Loan 4							
Loan 5							

Refund & Overpayment Tracker Explanation

The **Refund & Overpayment Tracker** is designed to help you keep track of any **refunds** or **overpayments** related to your college expenses. Whether you've paid more than required for tuition, housing, or other fees, or you receive a refund from financial aid, this tool helps you stay organized. By recording **dates**, **amounts**, and **refund sources**, you can ensure that you are aware of any adjustments made to your account and any money you are entitled to receive back. This tracker also helps you manage **overpayments** from previous semesters, ensuring that you apply those funds correctly or request refunds when appropriate. The **status** section is useful for tracking the progress of any refunds in process, and the **notes** section can be used to record any relevant details or actions taken. Keeping an accurate record of your refunds and overpayments can help you avoid confusion and ensure your finances are in order.

Date	Refund Source	Amount	Status (Refund/ Overpayment)	Notes
Refund 1				
Refund 2				
Refund 3				
Refund 4				
Refund 5				

Semester Budget Planner Explanation

The **Semester Budget Planner** is a tool designed to help you **manage your finances** over the course of a semester. This planner allows you to list and categorize all your **income** and **expenses**, from **tuition** and **housing costs** to **books, supplies, personal expenses**, and **transportation**. It provides a clear structure for keeping track of your **monthly income** and **expenses**, ensuring you stay within your **budget**. By categorizing expenses, you can identify where you're spending the most and adjust accordingly to avoid overspending. The planner also allows you to set **financial goals**, track **payments**, and plan for **unexpected expenses**. Having a semester-long view of your finances helps you ensure that you're managing your money effectively and are prepared for any additional costs that may arise throughout the semester. This template is a practical way to maintain **financial stability** during your college journey.

Category	Planned Amount	Actual Amount	Difference	Notes
Tuition				
Housing				
Books & Supplies				
Transportation				

Category	Planned Amount	Actual Amount	Difference	Notes
Food/Meals				
Personal Expenses				
Entertainment				
Total Income				
Total Expenses				
Balance				

Monthly Expense Tracker Explanation

The **Monthly Expense Tracker** is a straightforward tool to help you track your **monthly spending** across various categories. By recording your **income** and **expenses** for each month, this tracker helps you stay on top of your financial situation and avoid overspending. Categories may include **tuition**, **housing**, **food**, **entertainment**, and **personal expenses**, among others. This tool provides a snapshot of your **monthly budget**, helping you see exactly where your money is going. The **balance** section allows you to track the difference between your income and expenses, giving you a clear view of whether you are living within your means or need to make adjustments. By using this tracker regularly, you can stay **financially disciplined**, ensure you don't go over budget, and plan ahead for future months. This is an essential tool for **students** or anyone managing a monthly budget to track their finances effectively.

Category	Planned Amount	Actual Amount	Difference	Notes
Tuition				
Housing				
Books & Supplies				
Transportation				
Food/Meals				
Personal Expenses				
Entertainment				
Total Income				
Total Expenses				
Balance				

Savings Goal Planner Explanation

The **Savings Goal Planner** is designed to help you set clear and **achievable savings goals** for your education, living expenses, or any other financial priorities. Whether you're saving for **tuition**, **books**, or **travel expenses**, this planner enables you to break down large savings goals into smaller, manageable targets. The template helps you set **target amounts** for each goal, track your **progress** over time, and identify the steps required to reach those targets. By establishing specific **timeframes** and **monthly savings targets**, you can ensure that you are consistently contributing toward your goals. This tool is essential for **maintaining focus** and ensuring that you have a clear strategy for saving over time. The planner also includes space for noting any **adjustments** you may need to make to your plan based on changes in your financial situation. With this tool, you can stay motivated and on track to reach your savings goals.

Savings Goal	Target Amount	Time-frame	Monthly Savings Target	Current Savings	Progress	Notes
Goal 1 (e.g., Tuition)						
Goal 2 (e.g., Books)						
Goal 3 (e.g., Emergency Fund)						
Goal 4						
Goal 5						

Emergency Fund Planning Explanation

The **Emergency Fund Planning** template is designed to help you establish an **emergency fund** for unexpected expenses during your college journey. An emergency fund is crucial for covering unplanned costs such as **medical bills**, **car repairs**, or other unforeseen expenses. This planning tool helps you determine how much you need to save for your **emergency fund** and track your **progress** toward building it. The planner includes sections for estimating **monthly contributions**, setting a **target savings goal**, and evaluating how much you can afford to save each month. It also helps you assess the **timeframe** needed to reach your goal. By planning ahead, you can ensure that you have a safety net in place for unexpected situations, reducing stress and financial strain. This template encourages proactive **financial planning** and ensures you're prepared for any emergencies that may arise.

Emergency Fund Target	Monthly Contribu-tion	Total Savings Goal	Current Savings	Time-frame	Progress	Notes
Emergency Fund 1 (e.g., Medical)						

Emergency Fund Target	Monthly Contribution	Total Savings Goal	Current Savings	Timeframe	Progress	Notes
Emergency Fund 2 (e.g., Car Repairs)						
Emergency Fund 3						
Emergency Fund 4						

Financial Aid Offer Comparison Explanation

The **Financial Aid Offer Comparison** template is designed to help you **evaluate and compare the financial aid offers** from different schools, ensuring that you make an informed decision about where to attend. When reviewing financial aid offers, it's essential to compare **scholarships**, **grants**, **loans**, and **work-study opportunities** side by side. This template allows you to track each **school's offer**, noting the **types of aid**, **award amounts**, and any **terms and conditions** attached. You can also track **remaining costs** (after aid) and compare how each school's offer stacks up in terms of overall affordability. This tool ensures that you clearly understand the **financial implications** of each offer and can make a decision that aligns with both your educational and financial goals. By breaking down the offers into key components, you can assess which school provides the best financial aid package for your needs.

School Name	Scholarships	Grants	Loans	Work-Study	Total Financial Aid	Remaining Cost	Notes
School 1							
School 2							
School 3							
School 4							
School 5							

Work-Study Planning Sheet Explanation

The **Work-Study Planning Sheet** is designed to help you plan and manage your **work-study** opportunities while attending college. Work-study programs are a great way to earn money while balancing academics, and this sheet allows you to track the details of your **work-study job**. The template includes sections for recording the **job title**, **work hours**, **earnings**, and any specific **responsibilities** or **tasks** associated with the job. This sheet helps you **balance work and school commitments**, ensuring that your job doesn't interfere with your **academic performance**. It also provides space to record **goals** for your work-study experience, such as gaining

work experience in a particular field, building your **resume**, or developing new **skills**. By keeping track of your work-study job, you can effectively manage your time, keep your earnings organized, and ensure you are meeting your **academic and financial goals**.

Job Title	Depart-ment	Work Hours	Hourly Wage	Weekly Earnings	Responsibili-ties/Tasks	Goals for This Job
Job 1						
Job 2						
Job 3						
Job 4						
Job 5						

Income & Side Job Tracker Explanation

The **Income & Side Job Tracker** template helps you manage your **additional sources of income**, such as **side jobs** or **freelance work**. Whether you're working part-time, freelancing, or running a small business, it's essential to keep track of your **earnings** to ensure that you're meeting your financial goals. This tracker allows you to list each **source of income**, record the **amount earned**, and monitor **payment schedules**. You can track **income received** on a weekly or monthly basis, ensuring that you are on top of all your earnings. The template also provides space to note any **expenses** related to your side job or freelance work, helping you calculate your **net earnings**. By staying organized and keeping a record of your additional income, you can better manage your finances and ensure that your side jobs contribute positively to your overall financial plan.

Source of Income	Amount Earned	Payment Date	Frequency (Weekly/ Monthly)	Expenses Related to Job	Net Income	Notes
Side Job 1						
Side Job 2						
Side Job 3						
Side Job 4						
Side Job 5						

Financial Reflection Page Explanation

The **Financial Reflection Page** is a tool for reflecting on your **financial journey** and assessing your **financial progress**. This template encourages you to think about your **spending habits**, **savings goals**, and overall financial **health**. The reflection page allows you to track important aspects such as **how well you're sticking to your budget**, whether you've reached your **savings targets**, and if you've encountered any financial **challenges**. By reflecting on your financial habits, you can identify areas where you're succeeding and areas that need improvement. This page is a great way to **review** your **spending** and **savings goals** periodically, allowing you to adjust your plan and make informed decisions about your **money management**. The reflection process helps you **stay motivated** and focused on your long-term **financial goals**, while ensuring that you are financially prepared for both **short-term expenses** and **future needs**.

How well have I stuck to my budget?

Answer:

Action Plan for Improvement:

Have I met my savings goals?

Answer:

Action Plan for Improvement:

What were my biggest financial challenges this month?

Answer:

Action Plan for Improvement:

What changes can I make to improve my financial habits?

Answer:

Action Plan for Improvement:

What is my biggest financial priority right now?

Answer:

Action Plan for Improvement:

What are my short-term and long-term financial goals?

Answer:

Action Plan for Improvement:

What steps will I take next to improve my financial situation?

Answer:

Action Plan for Improvement:

Section 5

Essay Planning & Writing Support

Understanding Scholarship Prompts

When applying for scholarships, one of the most critical components is responding to the essay prompts provided by the scholarship organization. Scholarship prompts typically ask you to reflect on your experiences, share your goals, or demonstrate your qualities, and they serve as an opportunity to show the selection committee who you are beyond your grades and resume. Understanding how to approach and effectively respond to scholarship prompts can significantly improve your chances of securing financial aid. In this guide, we will explore how to understand, interpret, and respond to scholarship essay prompts in a way that highlights your strengths, experiences, and potential.

Decoding the Prompt

The first step in responding to a scholarship essay prompt is decoding it. At first glance, a prompt might seem straightforward, but the key to writing a successful essay lies in understanding exactly what is being asked. Scholarship prompts vary widely in their approach, ranging from questions about personal challenges to more general queries about your career goals or community involvement. Here are some of the most common types of prompts you might encounter:

1. **Personal Experience**: These prompts often ask you to discuss a personal experience, challenge, or achievement. For example, "Describe a time when you overcame a significant obstacle." The goal is to highlight your resilience, problem-solving skills, and ability to navigate adversity. It's important to be authentic and choose an experience that truly represents your character.

2. **Future Goals**: Prompts that ask about your future goals or career aspirations are your chance to explain why you are pursuing your chosen field and how receiving the scholarship will help you achieve your objectives. For example, "What are your career goals, and how will this scholarship help you achieve them?" This is where you need to connect the dots between your academic journey, career path, and how the scholarship fits into your plans.

3. **Community Involvement**: Many scholarships value applicants who demonstrate a commitment to their community. A typical prompt could ask, "How have you contributed to your community, and why is community service important to you?" This type of prompt allows you to showcase your volunteer work, leadership roles, and how you've made a positive impact. Even if you haven't had extensive volunteer experiences, consider discussing any small efforts that demonstrate your character.

4. **Leadership and Initiative**: These prompts focus on your leadership qualities,

such as "Describe a time when you showed leadership skills." The goal is to demonstrate your ability to take initiative, guide others, and influence positive change. It's important to select an example where you **actively contributed** to a team or project, highlighting your role in achieving a goal.

5. **Creative and Abstract Questions**: Some prompts take a more abstract or **creative approach**, such as "If you could meet any historical figure, who would it be and why?" These questions allow you to show your **creativity**, **critical thinking**, and **personality**. While these types of prompts are less common, they give you the freedom to showcase your unique perspective.

Breaking Down the Prompt

After identifying the type of scholarship prompt, break it down into smaller, manageable parts. Identify the **key elements** and make sure to **address each part of the question**. If the prompt has multiple parts, it's easy to miss a crucial element if you rush through your response. For example, a question like "Explain your future career goals and how this scholarship will help you achieve them" can be broken down into two parts: 1) explaining your goals and 2) connecting the scholarship to your goals.

When reading the prompt, ask yourself these questions:

- What is the main topic or focus of the prompt?
- Are there multiple questions or sub-questions?
- What **specific qualities or experiences** is the prompt asking you to discuss?
- Is the prompt asking for a **personal story**, **future goals**, or a **demonstration of character**?

Once you've fully understood the prompt's requirements, take some time to **brainstorm** ideas and choose the best response that fits within the scholarship's framework.

Planning Your Response

The next step is **planning your response**. Writing a scholarship essay is a lot like writing any other essay – it requires **structure**. Organize your thoughts before you begin writing to ensure that your response is clear, concise, and well-organized. A good essay will follow a simple structure:

1. **Introduction**: Start by introducing the topic and providing a **brief overview** of what you will discuss. Make sure to grab the reader's attention from the very first sentence. A compelling introduction can make a big difference in how the selection committee perceives your essay.

2. **Body Paragraphs**: The body of your essay should **expand on the main**

points you raised in the introduction. Each paragraph should cover a specific idea or example that answers the prompt in detail. Be sure to provide **concrete examples** from your life, studies, or experiences that demonstrate the traits, skills, or values the scholarship committee is looking for.

3. **Conclusion**: Your conclusion should wrap up the essay by **reinforcing your main points**. Summarize why you are a strong candidate for the scholarship and how receiving it will help you achieve your goals. Leave the reader with a lasting impression of who you are and why you deserve the scholarship.

Tips for Writing a Strong Response

- **Be Authentic**: One of the most important aspects of a strong scholarship essay is being **genuine**. Don't try to tell the committee what you think they want to hear. Instead, focus on your **true experiences** and goals.
- **Show, Don't Tell**: Rather than simply stating your qualities or accomplishments, **demonstrate them** through specific examples. Instead of saying "I am a dedicated student," you could write, "Last semester, I balanced a full course load with volunteer work at the local food bank, maintaining a 3.8 GPA."
- **Stay Focused**: Keep your response focused on answering the prompt. Avoid straying into unrelated topics or rambling. Stay concise and clear throughout your essay.
- **Proofread and Edit**: Once you've written your essay, **proofread** it several times. Look for spelling and grammar errors, but also check for clarity and structure. Ask someone else to review your essay as well, as they may catch mistakes you missed.

Conclusion

Understanding and responding to scholarship prompts effectively is essential for crafting a compelling scholarship application. By carefully **decoding the prompt**, **organizing your thoughts**, and **writing a focused response**, you can create an essay that stands out. Remember that scholarship essays are not just about answering questions; they're about **showcasing who you are**, your experiences, and your future goals in a way that resonates with the scholarship committee. The more effort you put into understanding and addressing the prompt, the better your chances of securing the financial support you need for your education.

Essay Brainstorming Worksheet Template

The **Essay Brainstorming Worksheet** is designed to help you organize your thoughts and generate ideas for your scholarship essays. The first column is for the **essay prompt or topic**, so you can clearly see what the scholarship asks for. In the second column, jot down the **main idea or message** you want to convey in your essay. This is the central theme or message that you want the committee to understand about you. The third column is for **supporting examples or experiences**. These are real-life events, achievements, or challenges you can reference to demonstrate your strengths and fit for the scholarship. Lastly, the **key points to include** column allows you to list the **specific points** you want to cover, ensuring your essay stays focused and coherent. This worksheet helps structure your brainstorming process and ensures that you don't overlook any essential elements while writing your essay.

Essay Prompt	Main Idea	Supporting Examples	Key Points to Include
1			
2			
3			
4			
5			
6			
7			
8			
9			
10			

Personal Story Mapping Template

The **Personal Story Mapping** template helps you plan and organize the **personal story** you'll use to illustrate your qualifications, experiences, and values in your scholarship essay. In the first column, write a **brief description of the personal story** or experience you plan to share. This could be an achievement, challenge, or significant moment in your life. The second column should detail the **key event or experience** within your story, highlighting the most significant moments or actions. The third column focuses on the **emotions and challenges faced** during the experience. This is where you describe your **personal struggles**, obstacles, or feelings during the event, which helps humanize your story and makes it more relatable. Finally, the **outcome or impact** column is where you note how the experience **shaped you**, what you learned, and how it **impacted your personal growth**. This template helps you outline your story effectively, ensuring that you capture all the essential elements that showcase your qualities for the scholarship committee.

Personal Story	Key Event/ Experience	Emotions/Challenges Faced	Outcome/ Impact
Scholarship 1			
Scholarship 2			
Scholarship 3			
Scholarship 4			
Scholarship 5			
Scholarship 6			

Personal Story	Key Event/ Experience	Emotions/Challenges Faced	Outcome/ Impact
Scholarship 7			
Scholarship 8			
Scholarship 9			
Scholarship 10			

Tone & Clarity Review Explanation

The **Tone & Clarity Review** template is designed to help you evaluate whether your scholarship essay **effectively communicates** your ideas while maintaining the appropriate tone and clarity. The tone of your essay plays a significant role in how your message is perceived by the scholarship committee. Whether your tone is **formal, personal, or inspirational**, it needs to align with the goals of the essay and the scholarship requirements. This template prompts you to review whether the tone is consistent throughout the essay, if it reflects your **personality** appropriately, and if it is engaging without being too casual or too stiff. Additionally, the review helps you evaluate the **clarity of your writing**—ensuring that your ideas are **organized**, **clear**, and easy to understand. By using this template, you can identify areas where your writing might be confusing or overly complex, and make revisions to improve readability and impact. This review process helps you refine your essay to make it both **compelling** and **clear** to the reader.

Element	Yes/No	Comments/Suggestions for Improvement
Is the tone consistent throughout the essay?		

Element	Yes/No	Comments/Suggestions for Improvement
Does the tone align with the scholarship's focus?		
Is the tone appropriate for the scholarship audience?		
Are the ideas clearly organized?		
Are the ideas easy to understand?		
Are there any confusing or unclear sections?		
Does the introduction grab the reader's attention?		
Is the conclusion strong and impactful?		

Grammar & Proofreading Sheet Explanation

The **Grammar & Proofreading Sheet** is an essential tool for ensuring that your scholarship essay is free of **spelling, grammar, and punctuation errors**. Even the most brilliant ideas can be overlooked if they are presented in poorly written, error-ridden text. This sheet encourages a **detailed review** of your essay's **grammar**, **spelling**, and **punctuation** to ensure that it adheres to proper writing conventions. It guides you through checking sentence structure, **verb tense**, **subject-verb agreement**, and **pronoun usage**, which are common areas where mistakes can occur. The template also includes space for **notes** on recurring issues or areas that need special attention during the proofreading process. By systematically reviewing your essay for these errors, you ensure that your final draft is polished and professional. This proofreading process not only improves the clarity of your writing but also **enhances your credibility** by demonstrating your attention to detail and commitment to producing high-quality work.

Area to Check	Yes/ No	Issues Found (If Any)	Action Needed
Sentence Structure			
Verb Tense Consistency			
Subject-Verb Agreement			

Area to Check	Yes/ No	Issues Found (If Any)	Action Needed
Pronoun Usage			
Punctuation			
Spelling			
Capitalization			
Clarity of Sentences			
Use of Transition Words			
Consistency of Formatting			

Feedback & Revision Notes Explanation

The **Feedback & Revision Notes** template is designed to help you **organize feedback** you receive on your scholarship essays and track the necessary **revisions**. After writing your initial draft, seeking feedback from **teachers**, **mentors**, or **peers** is an important step. The feedback you receive can be used to improve your essay's clarity, tone, structure, and overall effectiveness. This template helps you document the **specific feedback** you received, including suggestions for improving your essay. You can list the **areas to revise** (such as organization, grammar, or content) and then outline your **action plan for revisions** in the next column. This ensures that you are addressing all necessary changes before finalizing your essay. The feedback section provides a clear record of changes made, and the revision steps help keep your edits organized and focused. By tracking feedback and revisions systematically, you ensure that your essay evolves into its best form before submission.

Feedback Area	Feedback/ Comment	Revision Steps/ Actions	Status/Notes
Content			
Organization			
Clarity			
Grammar/ Spelling			
Tone/Voice			

Feedback Area	Feedback/ Comment	Revision Steps/ Actions	Status/Notes
Specific Suggestions			
Overall Strengths			

Final Submission Checklist Explanation

The **Final Submission Checklist** template is a crucial tool to ensure that your scholarship application is **complete** and **correct** before submission. Applying for scholarships often involves several components, including **essays, recommendation letters**, **transcripts**, and **supporting documents**. This checklist helps you ensure that all required materials have been **prepared**, **reviewed**, and **submitted** on time. The template includes specific tasks to review, such as **double-checking essay formatting**, ensuring your **recommendation letters** are submitted, and confirming that you've followed all **submission guidelines**. By checking off each item on the list, you can avoid mistakes, like missing documents or incorrect formatting, that could affect your application. The checklist serves as a final, comprehensive review, ensuring that every detail is covered and that your application is ready to go. This step is essential for submitting a polished, complete application that stands out to scholarship committees.

Task	Completed (Yes/No)	Date Completed	Notes
Review for clarity			
Check word count			
Ensure formatting			
Proofread for grammar/ spelling			
Scholarship requirements met			
Required documents submitted			
Recommendation letters submitted			
Complete any necessary forms			
Submit application before deadline			

Section 6

Final Review, Accountability & Success Tracking

Scholarship Submission Summary Explanation

The **Scholarship Submission Summary** template helps you keep track of all the **scholarships** you've applied for, including the **required documents**, **submission dates**, and the **status** of your application. By organizing this information, you can easily see what's been submitted, what's still pending, and what additional materials or actions are required. This tracker includes columns to record details such as the **scholarship name**, **submission method**, and **deadline**, so you can stay on top of each application's requirements. It is especially useful if you are applying to multiple scholarships simultaneously, helping you avoid missing any important deadlines. By keeping all your submission information in one place, you can **track progress** and ensure that every scholarship is completed on time.

Scholarship Name	Submission Method	Required Documents	Deadline	Status (Submitted/ Pending)	Notes
1					
2					
3					
4					
5					

GPA Maintenance Plan Explanation

The **GPA Maintenance Plan** is a tool to help you track and maintain a strong **Grade Point Average (GPA)** throughout your academic career. Many scholarships require you to maintain a minimum GPA to **renew** your funding, and this plan helps you stay on track to meet those requirements. The template includes sections to set **GPA goals**, **track academic performance**, and plan strategies for **improvement** if your GPA starts to fall behind. You can record specific **study habits**, **time management techniques**, and **resources** you will use to maintain or improve your GPA. This plan helps ensure that you are **actively working** to meet scholarship requirements and can help you stay focused on achieving both **academic excellence** and **scholarship retention**.

Action/Goal	Target GPA	Deadline/Timeline	Action Steps

Semester GPA Goal				

Cumulative GPA Goal				

Study Habits Improvement				

Time Management Strategies				

Tutoring/Resources				

Action Plan for Improvement				

Scholarship Renewal Timeline Explanation

The **Scholarship Renewal Timeline** template is designed to help you **track scholarship renewal deadlines** and ensure you meet all the **requirements** to maintain your scholarship each year. Many scholarships require you to submit documentation or meet certain criteria to renew your funding, such as maintaining a certain **GPA**, completing **community service hours**, or submitting **progress reports**. This timeline helps you plan ahead by recording important **dates** and **action steps** required for renewal. The template allows you to break down the process into **yearly tasks**, ensuring that you have enough time to gather documents, complete required actions, and submit everything before the deadlines. This timeline helps you stay on top of your **scholarship renewal responsibilities**, preventing you from missing any important steps that could affect your funding.

Scholarship Name	Renewal Deadline	Required Documents/ Actions	Status	Notes
Scholarship 1				
Scholarship 2				
Scholarship 3				
Scholarship 4				
Scholarship 5				

opportunities, you can develop strategies to **stay on track** for future applications and improve your approach to **time management**, **research**, or **organization**. This review not only helps you **learn from past mistakes** but also empowers you to **take proactive steps** toward improving your chances of success in the future.

Missed Opportunity	Reason	Lessons Learned	Action Plan for Future
1			
2			
3			
4			
5			

Lessons Learned Reflection Explanation

The **Lessons Learned Reflection** template is designed to help you evaluate the **lessons** you've learned throughout your scholarship application journey or academic pursuits. Whether you faced challenges in managing your time, missed key deadlines, or encountered unexpected obstacles, this template allows you to **reflect on those experiences** and turn them into valuable lessons for the future. The worksheet encourages you to think about **what worked**, **what didn't**, and what adjustments you can make going forward. It helps you evaluate your **progress**, **successes**, and areas for growth, so you can continue to **develop** and **improve** your strategies for future scholarship applications. By reflecting on what you've learned, you can become more **efficient**, **resilient**, and prepared for the next steps in your academic and financial journey.

Experience	What Went Well	What Didn't Go Well	Lessons Learned	Action Plan for Future
1				
2				
3				
4				
5				

Motivation Check-In Explanation

The **Motivation Check-In** template is designed to help you assess your **motivation levels** during the scholarship application process or throughout your academic work. Staying motivated is essential when applying for multiple scholarships, managing academic work, and navigating financial responsibilities. This check-in template encourages you to **reflect on your motivation**, identify any **challenges** or **distractions**, and evaluate your **progress** toward achieving your goals. It includes sections for identifying **what's driving you**, **how confident you feel about your**

progress, and **how to overcome obstacles**. This tool allows you to assess whether you need to adjust your goals, break tasks into smaller steps, or find new ways to stay inspired. Regular motivation check-ins help ensure you stay focused, **keep momentum**, and **remain positive** throughout the application and college journey.

Motivation Level (1-10)	What's Motivating Me	Challenges/ Obstacles	Progress	Next Steps	Notes

Long-Term Education Vision Explanation

The **Long-Term Education Vision** template is a tool designed to help you **define and track your long-term educational goals**. Education is not just about completing a degree—it's about shaping your future and understanding the bigger picture of how education aligns with your life goals. This vision template encourages you to think about your **ultimate educational aspirations**, including **degrees** or **programs** you want to pursue, **fields of study** that interest you, and how education fits into your broader **career** and **personal development** goals. It also asks you to reflect on the **steps** and **resources** needed to achieve these goals, whether it's securing financial aid, researching specific schools, or gaining relevant experience. This long-term vision helps you stay **focused**, **motivated**, and **on track**, ensuring that your educational journey is aligned with your career and personal objectives. By setting a clear vision, you can avoid distractions and remain committed to achieving your educational aspirations.

Educational Goals	Degree/ Program	Timeline	Steps to Achieve Goal	Resources Needed	Obstacles & Challenges	Notes
Goal 1						
Goal 2						
Goal 3						
Goal 4						
Goal 5						

Career Path Reflection Explanation

The **Career Path Reflection** template encourages you to reflect on your **career journey** and assess the **path** you are on, the **goals** you have, and the **steps** you need to take to achieve them. Whether you are just beginning your career, still in school, or considering a career change, this template helps you evaluate where you are and where you want to go. It asks you to identify your **career interests**, **skills**, and **experiences** that have shaped your path. This reflection also encourages you to think about **long-term career goals** and how your **education** and **professional experiences** contribute to reaching those goals. The template prompts you to consider any **barriers** you might face and how to overcome them, as well as the **actions** you need to take to get closer to your desired career. Regular reflection on your career path helps you stay focused on your professional growth and ensures that you are constantly working toward the career of your dreams.

Current Job/Role	Career Interests & Goals	Skills/ Experience Gained	Long-Term Career Aspirations	Steps to Achieve Career Goals	Obstacles & Barriers	Action Plan
Job/Role 1						
Job/Role 2						
Job/Role 3						
Job/Role 4						
Job/Role 5						

Section 7
Application Timelines

General Academic Merit Scholarships

Scholarship	Deadline
Ron Brown Scholar Program	January 9
GE-Reagan Foundation Scholarship Program	January 5
John F. Kennedy Profile in Courage Essay Contest	January
American Mensa Foundation Scholarship	January
Enjuris Future Leaders Scholarship	January
Elks National Foundation Legacy Awards	January
Davidson Fellows Scholarship	February
Discover Student Loans Scholarship Award	February
American Legion Legacy Scholarship (Need-Based Branch)	February
Ayn Rand Essay Contest "We the Living"	February
We the Students Essay Contest (Bill of Rights Institute)	February
Society of Mayflower Descendants Merit Award	March
Scholars Helping Collars Essay Scholarship	March
American Legion Legacy Scholarship	March
Phi Delta Kappa Prospective Educator Scholarship	March
Daughters of the American Revolution General Scholarship	March
Sons of the American Revolution Youth Contest Awards	March
American Legion Samsung American Legion Scholarship	March
Coca-Cola Leaders of Tomorrow Scholarship	March
John Locke Institute Essay Competition	April
National Sojourners Essay Contest	April
American Fire Sprinkler Association Scholarship Contest	April
American Legion Oratorical Contest Scholarship	April
Frame My Future Scholarship Contest	April
Leadership 1000 Scholarship	May
Imagine America Foundation Scholarship	May
Ayn Rand Essay Contest Scholarship	May
Vegetarian Resource Group Scholarship	April
Hagan Scholarship Foundation	April
National Honor Society Scholarship	April

Rolling Scholarships:

Scholarship	Deadline
Courage to Grow Scholarship	**Last day of each month**
Unigo $10K Scholarship	**Rolling (monthly)**
Cappex Easy College Money Scholarship	**Rolling (monthly)**
Niche "No Essay" Scholarship	**Rolling (monthly)**
ScholarshipPoints $10,000 Scholarship	**Rolling (monthly)**
Fastweb "Scholarship of the Month"	**Monthly**
Varsity Tutors College Scholarship Contest	**Monthly**
Chegg $1,000 Monthly Scholarship	**Monthly**
DoSomething.org Easy Scholarships	**Monthly**
Tallo Merit Scholarships	**Varies by year**
Be Bold "No Essay" Scholarship	**Rolling**
College JumpStart Scholarship	**October**

General Need-Based Scholarship

Scholarship	Deadline
Jack Kent Cooke Young Scholars Program (Need Focus for High Schoolers)	**January**
Robert F. Kennedy Urban Education Fund	**January**
Beyond 12 Scholarship Program	**January**
Educational Credit Management Corporation Foundation Awards	**January**
Soros Fellowships for New Americans (Need-Inclusive)	**November**
Hispanic Scholarship Fund General Awards	**February 15**
American Indian College Fund Need-Based Scholarships	**February**
Thurgood Marshall College Fund Need-Based Scholarships	**February**
UNCF General Scholarship Program (Need-Based Focus)	**February**
Posse Foundation Scholarships	**February**
Gates Millennium Scholars Program (Need-Based Focus)	**February**
Western Union Foundation Global Scholarship	**February**
Children's Defense Fund Beat the Odds Scholarship	**February**
Kaplan Leadership Program	**February**
ScholarMatch Scholarships	**February**
America Needs You Fellowship and Scholarship	**February**
Say Yes to Education Scholarships	**March**
First Generation Foundation Need-Based Scholarship	**March**

Scholarship	Deadline
Society for Science STEM Talent Expansion Program (Need Component Awards)	**March**
Horatio Alger Career & Technical Scholarships (Need-Based)	**April**
Wells Fargo Scholarship Program for People with Disabilities (Need-Based Portion)	**April**
Davis-Putter Scholarship Fund	**March**
Horatio Alger National Career & Technical Program	**April**
Greenhouse Scholars Program	**April**
Educational Foundation of America Scholarship	**March**
Scholarship America Dream Award	**April**
iMentor College Scholarships	**March**
Phillips Foundation Need Scholarships	**March**
College Success Foundation Scholarships	**April**
Leadership for Educational Equity Need-Based Awards	**March**
Summer Search College Scholarships	**May**
Kaplan Test Prep Scholarships for Low-Income Students	**April**
Rosen Scholarship Fund	**May**
Peter Thiel Foundation Scholarships	**May**
A Better Chance College Preparatory Scholarships	**May**
KIPP Through College Scholarships	**April**
College Track Scholarships	**April**
Greenhouse Scholars Colorado Program	**April**
College Advising Corps Awards	**May**
SEO Scholars Program	**May**
Breakthrough Collaborative Scholarships	**April**
Minds Matter National Scholarship	**May**
Bright Prospect College Access Scholarship	**March**
All Stars Project Scholarship	**March**
J. Craig Venter Foundation Scholarships	**March**
Leonore Annenberg Scholarship Fund	**Sept**
Michael & Susan Dell Foundation Scholars Program (Need Branch)	**Sept**
College Point Advising Program Scholarships	**Sept**
Coca-Cola First-Generation Need-Based Scholarship	**Sept**
United States Achievement Academy Need-Based Awards	**Sept**
College Success Foundation Scholarships	**April**

Scholarship	Deadline
Kaplan Educational Foundation Scholarships	**March**
UNCF/Koch Scholars Program (Need-Inclusive)	**Oct**
College Board Opportunity Scholarships (Need Emphasis)	**Oct**
QuestBridge National College Match	**Sept 30**
Leonore Annenberg Scholarship Fund	**Sept**

Rolling Scholarships:

Scholarship	Deadline
Courage to Grow Scholarship	Last day of each month
Unigo $10K Scholarship	Rolling (monthly)
Cappex Easy College Money Scholarship	Rolling (monthly)
Niche "No Essay" Scholarship	Rolling (monthly)
ScholarshipPoints $10,000 Scholarship	Rolling (monthly)
Fastweb "Scholarship of the Month"	Monthly
Varsity Tutors College Scholarship Contest	Monthly
Chegg $1,000 Monthly Scholarship	Monthly
DoSomething.org Easy Scholarships	Monthly
Tallo Merit Scholarships	Varies by year
Be Bold "No Essay" Scholarship	Rolling
College JumpStart Scholarship	October2025

STEM & Engineering Scholarships

Scholarship	Deadline
Barry Goldwater Scholarship	**January 30**
Jack Kent Cooke Young Scholars Program (Need Focus for High Schoolers)	**January**
Robert F. Kennedy Urban Education Fund	**January**
Beyond 12 Scholarship Program	**January**
Educational Credit Management Corporation Foundation Awards	**January**
Soros Fellowships for New Americans (Need-Inclusive)	**November**
Hispanic Scholarship Fund General Awards	**February 15**
American Indian College Fund Need-Based Scholarships	**February**
Thurgood Marshall College Fund Need-Based Scholarships	**February**
UNCF General Scholarship Program (Need-Based Focus)	**February**
Posse Foundation Scholarships	**February**
Gates Millennium Scholars Program (Need-Based Focus)	**February**
Western Union Foundation Global Scholarship	**February**
Children's Defense Fund Beat the Odds Scholarship	**February**
Kaplan Leadership Program	**February**
ScholarMatch Scholarships	**February**
America Needs You Fellowship and Scholarship	**February**
Say Yes to Education Scholarships	**March**
First Generation Foundation Need-Based Scholarship	**March**
Society for Science STEM Talent Expansion Program (Need Component Awards)	**March**
Horatio Alger Career & Technical Scholarships (Need-Based)	**April**
Wells Fargo Scholarship Program for People with Disabilities (Need-Based Portion)	**April**
Davis-Putter Scholarship Fund	**March**
Horatio Alger National Career & Technical Program	**April**
Greenhouse Scholars Program	**April**
Educational Foundation of America Scholarship	**March**
Scholarship America Dream Award	**April**
iMentor College Scholarships	**March**
Phillips Foundation Need Scholarships	**March**
College Success Foundation Scholarships	**April**
Leadership for Educational Equity Need-Based Awards	**March**
Summer Search College Scholarships	**May**

Scholarship	Deadline
Kaplan Test Prep Scholarships for Low-Income Students	**April**
Rosen Scholarship Fund	**May**
Peter Thiel Foundation Scholarships	**May**
A Better Chance College Preparatory Scholarships	**May**
KIPP Through College Scholarships	**April**
College Track Scholarships	**April**
Greenhouse Scholars Colorado Program	**April**
College Advising Corps Awards	**May**
SEO Scholars Program	**May**
Breakthrough Collaborative Scholarships	**April**
Minds Matter National Scholarship	**May**
Bright Prospect College Access Scholarship	**March**
All Stars Project Scholarship	**March**
J. Craig Venter Foundation Scholarships	**March**
Leonore Annenberg Scholarship Fund	**Sept**
Michael & Susan Dell Foundation Scholars Program (Need Branch)	**Sept**
College Point Advising Program Scholarships	**Sept**
Coca-Cola First-Generation Need-Based Scholarship	**Sept**
United States Achievement Academy Need-Based Awards	**Sept**
College Success Foundation Scholarships	**April**
Kaplan Educational Foundation Scholarships	**March**
UNCF/Koch Scholars Program (Need-Inclusive)	**Oct**
College Board Opportunity Scholarships (Need Emphasis)	**Oct**
QuestBridge National College Match	**Sept 30**
Leonore Annenberg Scholarship Fund	**Sept**

Medical & Health Professions Scholarships – 75

Scholarship	Deadline
Tylenol Future Care Scholarship	**Aug 1**
Tylenol Future Care Health Professional Award	**Aug 1**
U.S. Army Health Professions Scholarship Program	**March**
U.S. Navy Health Professions Scholarship Program	**March**
U.S. Air Force Health Professions Scholarship Program	**March**
Mayo Clinic College of Medicine Scholarships	**March**
Cleveland Clinic Lerner College of Medicine Scholarships	**March**

Scholarship	Deadline
Johns Hopkins University School of Medicine Scholarships	**March**
Harvard Medical School General Scholarships	**March**
Yale School of Medicine Scholarships	**March**
Stanford School of Medicine Scholarships	**March**
University of California San Francisco Health Professions Scholarships	**March**
University of Michigan Medical School Scholarships	**March**
Duke University School of Nursing Scholarships	**March**
Columbia University School of Public Health Scholarships	**March**
University of North Carolina Gillings School of Public Health Scholarships	**March**
University of Washington School of Medicine Scholarships	**March**
Emory University School of Nursing Scholarships	**March**
University of Pennsylvania Perelman School of Medicine Scholarships	**March**
University of Chicago Pritzker School of Medicine Scholarships	**March**
Vanderbilt University School of Medicine Scholarships	**March**
Washington University in St. Louis School of Medicine Scholarships	**March**
Baylor College of Medicine Scholarships	**March**
National Health Service Corps (NHSC) Scholarship Program	**February**
Indian Health Service (IHS) Scholarship Program	**February 28**
National Medical Fellowships (NMF) Scholarships	**February**
American Medical Association (AMA) Foundation Minority Scholars Award	**February**
American Medical Women's Association (AMWA) Scholarships	**February**
American Dental Association (ADA) Foundation Scholarships	**February**
American Dental Education Association (ADEA) Scholarships	**February**
American Association of Colleges of Nursing (AACN) Scholarships	**February**
National Student Nurses' Association (NSNA) Foundation Scholarships	**February**
American Association of Nurse Practitioners (AANP) Scholarships	**February**
Johnson & Johnson Nursing Scholarships	**February**
March of Dimes Graduate Nursing Scholarships	**February**
Oncology Nursing Society Foundation Scholarships	**February**
American Academy of Nursing Scholarships	**February**

Scholarship	Deadline
Emergency Nurses Association Foundation Scholarships	**February**
National Black Nurses Association Scholarships	**February**
Hispanic Association of Colleges and Universities Nursing Scholarships	**February**
American Pharmacists Association Foundation Scholarships	**February**
American Society of Health-System Pharmacists (ASHP) Scholarships	**February**
American Association of Colleges of Pharmacy Scholarships	**February**
American Physical Therapy Association (APTA) Scholarships	**February**
American Occupational Therapy Foundation (AOTF) Scholarships	**February**
American Speech-Language-Hearing Foundation Scholarships	**February**
American Optometric Association (AOA) Scholarships	**February**
American Association of Colleges of Osteopathic Medicine (AACOM) Scholarships	**February**
American Academy of Physician Associates (AAPA) Scholarships	**February**
American College of Surgeons Scholarships	**February**
American Academy of Pediatrics Scholarships	**February**
American Academy of Family Physicians Foundation Scholarships	**February**
American College of Obstetricians and Gynecologists Scholarships	**February**
American Psychiatric Association Fellowships	**February**
American Psychological Association (APA) Scholarships and Fellowships	**February**
Psi Chi Honor Society Psychology Scholarships	**February**
American Counseling Association Foundation Scholarships	**February**
American Public Health Association (APHA) Scholarships	**February**
Association of Schools and Programs of Public Health Scholarships	**February**
Kaiser Permanente Health Equity Scholarships	**February**
CVS Health Minority Scholarship for Pharmacy Students	**February**
Walgreens Diversity Scholarship for Pharmacy Students	**February**
Dr. Pepper Tuition Giveaway (Healthcare Branch Awards)	**Dec**
National Hispanic Health Foundation Scholarships	**February**
National Association of Hispanic Nurses Scholarships	**February**
National Black MBA Healthcare Administration Scholarships	**February**
Abbott Nutrition Health Sciences Scholarships	**February**
Medtronic Foundation Scholarships	**February**
Boston Scientific Health Professions Scholarships	**February**
Johnson & Johnson Global Health Scholars	**February**

Scholarship	Deadline
United Health Foundation Diversity in Health Scholarship	**February**
American College of Healthcare Executives (ACHE) Scholarships	**February**
Association of University Programs in Health Administration Scholarships	**February**
National Association of Health Services Executives Scholarships	**February**
Health Resources and Services Administration (HRSA) Nursing Scholarships	**February**

Business & Economics Scholarships

Scholarship	Deadline
Deloitte Foundation Accounting Scholarship	**March 1 or March 15 (varies by participating school deadlines)**
Chartered Financial Analyst (CFA) Institute Scholarships (Student)	**Jul 31 (Student Scholarship) s**
Chartered Financial Analyst (CFA) Institute Scholarships (Professor)	**Jul 15 (Professor Scholarship)**
Chartered Financial Analyst (CFA) Institute Access Scholarship	**Multiple windows in (for November exam: 11 Feb–3 March)**
Ernst & Young (EY) Scholarship Program	**April 15 (anticipated annual window)**

Education & Teaching Scholarships

Scholarship	Deadline
American Federation of Teachers (AFT) Union Plus Scholarship	**January 31**
Phi Delta Kappa Prospective Educator Scholarship	**March 1**
National Council of Teachers of Mathematics (NCTM) Scholarships/Grants	**May 1**
Phi Delta Kappa Prospective Educator Scholarship (Teach.org variant)	**October31**
National Education Association (NEA) Foundation Scholarships	**TBD (Not yet published)**
Teacher Education Assistance for College and Higher Education (TEACH) Grant	**FAFSA deadline / campus dependent**

Arts & Humanities Scholarships

Scholarship	Deadline
The NinetyNines Amelia Earhart Memorial Scholarships	January 1
The NinetyNines First Wings Award	January 1
AIAA Undergraduate Scholarships	January 31
AIAA Graduate Awards	January 31
United Airlines Flight Operations Scholarship	February 15
AOPA Foundation High School Flight Training Scholarship	February 10
AOPA Foundation Teacher Flight Training Scholarship	February 10
American Airlines Education Foundation Scholarships	February 28
National Health Service Corps (NHSC) Scholarship Program	February
Indian Health Service (IHS) Scholarship Program	February 28
Women in Aviation International Scholarships	October 12
UAA Janice K. Barden Aviation Scholarship	October 15
NBAA William M. Fanning Maintenance Scholarship	July 31
NBAA Hank Hilsmann Memorial Scholarship	July 31
EAA Flight Training Scholarships	May 1
EAA PostSecondary Scholarships	March 1
Aero Club of New England Scholarships	March 1
Boeing Company Aviation Scholarship	March 1
Air Line Pilots Association Scholarship	April 1
Aircraft Electronics Association Foundation Scholarships	April 1
PAMA Aviation Maintenance Scholarships	April 30
Bombardier Aerospace Scholarships	April 30
Pratt & Whitney Engine Scholarships	April 30
Embraer North America Scholarships	April 15
Lockheed Martin Aerospace Scholarships	March 12
General Electric Aviation Scholarships	March 15
Southwest Airlines Scholarships	March 15
NetJets SkillPointe Scholarship	March 31
Northrop Grumman Aviation Awards	March 31
ISA+21 Women Airline Pilots Scholarships	November 1
Delta Air Lines Aviation Scholarship	December 15

Law & Public Policy Scholarships

Scholarship	Deadline
American Society of International Law Fellowships	January 31
International Bar Association Scholarships	February 15
Legal Aid Society Public Interest Scholarships	February 15
The NinetyNines Amelia Earhart Memorial Scholarships	January 1
The NinetyNines First Wings Award	January 1
Federal Circuit Historical Society Law Scholarship	May 15
AIAA Undergraduate Scholarships	January 31
AIAA Graduate Awards	January 31
Trial Lawyers of America Scholarships	March 15
American Bar Association (ABA) Legal Opportunity Scholarship Fund	March 1
Federal Circuit Bar Association Scholarships	April 30
American Constitution Society Public Interest Scholarship	March 15
American College of Trial Lawyers Scholarships	May 1
American College of Bankruptcy Scholarships	March 31
National LGBT Bar Association Scholarships	April 30
National Black MBA Healthcare Administration Scholarships	February 28
American Civil Liberties Union (ACLU) Legal Fellowships	TBD
Brennan Center for Justice Legal Fellowships	August 1
Equal Justice Works Fellowships	September 1
Skadden Fellowship Program	September 15
Soros Justice Fellowships	October 12
Thurgood Marshall Civil Rights Scholarship	March 31
NAACP Legal Defense Fund Law Scholarships	April 15
American College of Tax Counsel Scholarships	May 1
National Tax Association Law Scholarships	April 30
Hague Academy of International Law Fellowships	November 1
American Immigration Lawyers Association Scholarships	April 15
American Health Law Association Scholarships	March 15
American Academy of Matrimonial Lawyers Scholarships	April 30

Scholarship	Deadline
American College of Trust and Estate Counsel Scholarships	May 15
American Law Institute Scholarships	March 31
State Bar Association Merit Scholarships	TBD (varies by state)
National Criminal Justice Association Scholarships	April 15
American Correctional Association Scholarships	April 1
American Probation and Parole Association Scholarships	May 15
American Juvenile Justice Association Scholarships	April 30
National Legal Aid & Defender Association Scholarships	March 31
American Prosecutors Research Institute Scholarships	May 1
Police Benevolent Association Legal Studies Scholarships	April 15
American Judges Association Scholarships	June 1
National Judicial College Fellowships	June 15
American Association for Justice (AAJ) Trial Advocacy Scholarships	May 1
National Association for Public Defense Scholarships	March 31
National Association of Women Lawyers Scholarships	April 15
American Inns of Court Scholarships	TBD
American Intellectual Property Law Association (AIPLA) Scholarships	March 1
Intellectual Property Law Section of ABA Scholarships	April 1

Journalism & Communications Scholarships

Scholarship	**Deadline**
Association for Women in Sports Media Scholarships	**February 15**
White House Correspondents' Association Scholarships	**February 15**
Center for Public Integrity Fellowships	**February 1**
ESPN Journalism Scholarships	**February 28**
American Advertising Federation Communications Scholarships	**February 28**
National Press Club Journalism Scholarships	**March 15**

Scholarship	**Deadline**
NBC News Digital Journalism Scholarships	**March 15**
Wall Street Journal Journalism Scholarships	**March 15**
National Press Photographers Foundation Scholarships	**March 15**
ProPublica Investigative Journalism Scholarships	**March 1**
Investigative Reporters and Editors (IRE) Scholarships	**March 1**
Society for News Design Scholarships	**March 30**
American Society of News Editors Scholarships	**March 30**
Asian American Journalists Association (AAJA) Scholarships	**March 31**
CBS News Walter Cronkite Journalism Scholarship	**March 31**
Chicago Tribune Journalism Scholarships	**March 31**
National Scholastic Press Association Scholarships	**April 1**
Washington Press Club Foundation Scholarships	**April 1**
International Association of Business Communicators (IABC) Scholarships	**April 1**
ABC News Communications Fellowship	**April 15**
Society of Professional Journalists (SPJ) Scholarships	**April 15**
Radio Television Digital News Association (RTDNA) Scholarships	**May 31**
National Association of Black Journalists (NABJ) Scholarships	**April 15**
National Association of Hispanic Journalists (NAHJ) Scholarships	**April 30**
Society of News Design Scholarships	**April 30**
Fox News Media Scholarships	**May 1**
Native American Journalists Association (NAJA) Scholarships	**May 1**
Associated Collegiate Press Scholarships	**May 15**
Arthur W. Page Society Scholarships	**May 15**
National Bar Institute Scholarships	**May 15**
Solutions Journalism Network Scholarships	**Rolling deadlines**

Scholarship	Deadline
Online News Association (ONA) Scholarships	**April 15**
Poynter Institute Journalism Fellowships	**TBD (varies by program cycle)**
Knight Foundation Journalism Fellowships	**TBD (varies by program cycle)**
Nieman Fellowships for Journalism at Harvard	**December 1**
Fulbright Journalism Grants	**October 10**
Overseas Press Club Foundation Scholarships	**December 1**
Reuters Journalism Training Program Scholarships	**December 1**
Bloomberg Journalism Fellowship Program	**December 1**
Associated Press Journalism Fellowships	**December 1**
New York Times Fellowship Program	**November 1**
Los Angeles Times Journalism Fellowship	**October 1**
Boston Globe Journalism Fellowships	**October 15**
National Press Club Journalism Scholarships	**March 15**
Dow Jones News Fund Intern Scholarships	**November 15**

Technology & Computing Scholarships

Scholarship	Deadline
Amazon Future Engineer Scholarship	January
Cornell Tech PhD Fellowship	February 1
SWE Scholarship (Society of Women Engineers)	February
Intel Scholars in Technology	February
Microsoft Disability Scholarship (STEM/tech branch)	March
Oracle Academy Scholarships	March
Oracle Fellowship for Computer Science	March
Cisco Networking Academy Scholarships	April
Amazon Machine Learning Research Scholarship	April
Palantir Global Impact Scholarship	April
Palantir Women in Technology Scholarship	April
Hugging Face AI Research Scholarship	April
OpenAI Research Scholars Program	May
NVIDIA Deep Learning Institute Scholarship	Rolling
Meta (Facebook) Fellowship Program	September
Google Lime Scholarship	December

Scholarship	Deadline
Adobe Research Women-in-Technology Scholarship	November
IBM PhD Fellowship Program	October
Stanford CS PhD Fellowship	December
CMU SCS Presidential Fellowship	December 1
Georgia Tech College of Computing PhD Fellowship	December 1
UIUC Siebel Scholars Program (CS)	Spring (faculty nomination)
MIT EECS Graduate Fellowship	December 15
UW Allen School PhD Fellowship	December 15
Berkeley EECS Chancellor's Fellowship	December 15
Caltech CMS PhD Fellowship	December 15
Columbia CS Presidential Fellowship	December 15
Princeton CS Graduate Fellowship	December 15
Yale CS PhD Fellowship	December 15
Harvard SEAS PhD Fellowship	December
Brown CS PhD Fellowship	December 15
Michigan CSE PhD Fellowship	December 1
Purdue CS PhD Fellowship	December 15
USC Viterbi CS PhD Fellowship	December 15

Skilled Trades & Vocational Scholarships

Scholarship	**Deadline**
Mike Rowe Works Foundation Work Ethic Scholarship	**May**
American Welding Society Foundation Vocational Scholarships	**February**
National Association of Home Builders Construction Scholarships	**March**
Associated General Contractors of America Workforce Scholarships	**June**
Plumbing-Heating-Cooling Contractors Educational Foundation Scholarships	**May**
National Electrical Contractors Association Scholarships	**April**
International Brotherhood of Electrical Workers (IBEW) Scholarships	**May**
Sheet Metal Workers International Association Scholarships	**May**
International Union of Operating Engineers Scholarships	**June**
Bricklayers and Allied Craftworkers Union Scholarships	**May**
United Brotherhood of Carpenters Scholarships	**March**
International Association of Machinists Scholarships	**February**
American Institute of Constructors Scholarships	**March**

Scholarship	Deadline
American Technical Education Association Scholarships	**February**
National Association of Trade and Technical Schools Scholarships	**March**
National Center for Construction Education and Research Scholarships	**May**
SkillsUSA Technical Scholarships	**February**
Automotive Service Excellence Foundation Scholarships	**March**
ASE/NATEF Automotive Technician Scholarships	**April**
DEWALT Trades Scholarship	**July 31**
John Deere Ag & Tech Vocational Scholarships	**March**
Ford Automotive Technician Scholarship	**April**
Toyota Technical Education Scholarship	**March**
FCA Foundation Scholarships	**April 15**
Harley-Davidson Technical Training Scholarship	**May**

Athletics & Sports Scholarships

Scholarship	Deadline
USA Gymnastics Academic All-American Award	**March**
USA Track & Field Foundation Scholarships	**Varies**
USA Wrestling Academic All-American Scholarship	**Spring**
National Strength and Conditioning Association Scholarships	**February**
U.S. Figure Skating Scholarships	**February**
United States Golf Association (USGA) Foundation Scholarships	**February**
National Junior Tennis and Learning Scholarships	**Varies**
National Interscholastic Athletic Administrators Association Scholarships	**February**
Professional Golfers' Association (PGA) Scholarships	**March**
Foot Locker Scholar Athletes Program	**December**
High School Heisman Scholarship	**October**
National Dairy Shrine Scholarships	**April**
USA Baseball Scholarship Program	**Spring**
Billie Jean King Leadership Initiative Scholarship	**Varies**
Muhammad Ali Sports Leadership Scholarship	**Spring**
Jackie Joyner-Kersee Foundation Athletic Scholarship	**Spring**
Babe Ruth League Scholarship	**May**
Little League International Scholarship	**Varies**

Scholarship	Deadline
Pop Warner Football Scholarship	**Spring**
National Cheerleading Association Scholarships	**Spring**
Dance Team Union Scholarships	**Spring**
NBA Cares Foundation Scholarships	**Spring**
WNBA Foundation Scholarships	**Spring**
National Lacrosse League Scholarships	**Spring**
U.S. Ski and Snowboard Association Scholarships	**Spring**
Rodeo Association of America Scholarships	**Spring**
NASCAR Foundation Scholarships	**Spring**
National Motorsports Press Association Scholarships	**Spring**
Ironman Foundation Triathlon Scholarships	**Spring**
Spartan Race Foundation Scholarships	**Spring**
Special Olympics USA Athlete Scholarships	**Varies**
Paralympic Athlete Scholarships	**Varies**
U.S. Olympic & Paralympic Foundation Scholarships	**Varies**
National Hockey League Foundation Scholarships	**Varies**
National Motorsports Press Association Scholarships	**Spring**
NCAA Postgraduate Scholarship Program	**Varies by sports season (fall, winter, spring)**
NAIA Scholar-Athlete Scholarships	**Set by participating NAIA colleges**
NJCAA Athletic Scholarships	**Varies by institution**
Gatorade Player of the Year Scholarship	**By nomination only**

Music & Performing Arts Scholarships

Scholarship	Deadline
National Flute Association Scholarships	**February**
Broadcast Music Inc. (BMI) Foundation Scholarships	**February**
Hal Leonard Vocal Competition Scholarships	**February**
National Association of Teachers of Singing Scholarships	**Varies by competition**
Percussive Arts Society Scholarships	**March**

Scholarship	Deadline
International Trumpet Guild Scholarships	**March**
Screen Actors Guild-American Federation of Television and Radio Artists (SAG-AFTRA) Scholarships	**March**
Writers Guild of America Foundation Scholarships (performing arts writing)	**Varies**
American Guild of Organists Scholarships	**April**
American Harp Society Scholarships	**April**
Songwriters Hall of Fame Scholarships	**April**
Academy of Television Arts & Sciences Foundation Scholarships	**Spring**
Actors' Equity Foundation Scholarships	**Spring**
Motion Picture Association Foundation Scholarships	**Spring**
Directors Guild of America Scholarships	**Spring**
Berklee College of Music Scholarships	**Varies**
Juilliard School Scholarships	**Varies**
Curtis Institute of Music Scholarships	**Varies**
Manhattan School of Music Scholarships	**Varies**
National Dance Education Organization Scholarships	**May**
National Association of Music Merchants (NAMM) Foundation Scholarships	**May**
Chopin Foundation of the United States Scholarships	**May**
Jazz at Lincoln Center Scholarships	**Spring**
Alvin Ailey American Dance Theater Scholarships	**Varies**
Martha Graham Dance Company Scholarships	**Varies**
School of American Ballet Scholarships	**Varies**
American Ballet Theatre Scholarships	**Varies**
Joffrey Ballet School Scholarships	**Varies**
Dance Theatre of Harlem Scholarships	**Spring**
Sphinx Competition Scholarships (classical music emphasis)	**October**
YoungArts National Arts Competition Scholarships (music branch)	**October**
Opera America Scholarships	**October**
International Clarinet Association Scholarships	**Spring**
International Viola Society Scholarships	**Spring**
International Federation of Actors Scholarships	**Varies**
National Federation of Music Clubs Scholarships	**Varies**

Scholarship	Deadline
Music Teachers National Association (MTNA) Scholarships	**Varies by competition**
American Choral Directors Association Scholarships	**Varies**
American Bandmasters Association Scholarships	**Varies**
American String Teachers Association Scholarships	**Spring**
Piano Technicians Guild Scholarships	**Varies**
American Society of Composers, Authors and Publishers (ASCAP) Foundation Scholarships	**Varies**
Babe Ruth League Scholarship	**May**

Visual Arts & Design Scholarships

Scholarship	Deadline
Society of Illustrators Scholarships	**February**
Rhode Island School of Design Scholarships	**February**
Graphic Communications Education Foundation Scholarships	**March**
International Sculpture Center Student Awards	**March**
Industrial Designers Society of America Scholarships	**March**
Society for News Design Scholarships (visual journalism branch)	**March**
Adobe Design Circle Scholarship	**March**
AIGA Worldstudio Scholarships	**April**
International Interior Design Association (IIDA) Foundation Scholarships	**April**
American Society of Interior Designers (ASID) Scholarships	**April**
Glass Art Society Scholarships	**Spring**
Textile Society of America Scholarships	**Spring**
National Art Honor Society Visual Arts Scholarships	**Spring**
National Society of Arts and Letters Visual Arts Scholarships	**Spring**
Surface Design Association Scholarships	**Varies**
National Art Education Association Scholarships	**October**
National Council on Education for the Ceramic Arts Scholarships	**October**
YoungArts National Arts Competition (visual arts branch)	**October**
Alliance for Young Artists & Writers Scholastic Art Awards	**December**
Art Renewal Center Scholarship Competition	**May**
School of Visual Arts Scholarships	**Varies**
Savannah College of Art and Design Scholarships	**Varies**
Pratt Institute Scholarships	**Varies**

Scholarship	Deadline
Maryland Institute College of Art Scholarships	**Varies**
California Institute of the Arts Scholarships	**Varies**

Literature & Writing Scholarships

Scholarship	Deadline
National Council of Teachers of English (NCTE) Achievement Awards in Writing	**February**
Iowa Young Writers Studio Scholarships	**February**
Academy of American Poets Student Poetry Prize	**March**
American Library Association Student Writing Award	**March**
Kenyon Review Young Writers Workshop Scholarships	**March**
Ayn Rand Institute Essay Contest (literature branch)	**April**
Signet Classics Student Essay Contest	**April**
Ruth Lilly and Dorothy Sargent Rosenberg Poetry Fellowships	**April**
Poetry Foundation Young Poets Prize	**Spring**
Shakespeare Society of America Scholarships	**Spring**
Poets & Writers Foundation Scholarships	**Spring**
Columbia Scholastic Press Association Writing Awards	**Spring**
Society of Children's Book Writers and Illustrators Scholarships	**Varies**
Bennington College Young Writers Awards	**November**
Patricia Grodd Poetry Prize for Young Writers	**November**
Foyle Young Poets of the Year Award (U.S. eligible)	**July**
YoungArts National Arts Competition (writing branch)	**October**
Scholastic Art & Writing Awards (writing branch)	**December**
National Novemberel Writing Month (NaNoWriMo) Young Writers Scholarship	**December**
Fine Arts Work Center Fellowships (literary track)	**December**
PEN America Writing Fellowships	**Varies by fellowship**
Association of Writers & Writing Programs (AWP) Scholarships	**Varies by program**
Sarah Lawrence College Writing Institute Scholarships	**Varies**
National Federation of State Poetry Societies Scholarships	**Varies**

Special Hobbies & Niche Interests Scholarships

Scholarship	Deadline
National Garden Clubs Scholarships	**February**
Orchid Society of America Scholarships	**March**
U.S. Chess Federation Scholarships	**April**
American Contract Bridge League Youth Scholarships	**May**
National Beekeepers Association Scholarships	**Spring**
Twitch Student Esports Scholarships	**Spring**
Anime Expo Foundation Scholarships	**Spring**
Comic-Con International Art & Fandom Scholarship	**Spring**
National Scrabble Association Scholarships	**Varies**
American Kennel Club (AKC) Junior Showmanship Scholarships	**November**
Cat Fanciers' Association Scholarships	**July**
American Rose Society Scholarships	**June**
Cosplay America Scholarship Fund	**Summer**
Star Wars Fan Scholarship Program	**Summer**
Blizzard Entertainment Esports Scholarships	**Varies**
Epic Games Esports Scholarships	**Varies**
Rubik's Cube World Organization Scholarships	**Varies**
Drone Racing League Scholarships	**Varies**
Robotics Education & Competition Foundation Scholarships	**Varies**
FIRST Robotics Competition Scholarships	**Varies**
VEX Robotics Scholarship Foundation	**Varies**
Esports Scholarship Foundation	**Varies**
Riot Games Esports Scholarships	**Varies**
Board Game Studies Association Scholarships	**Varies**
Science Fiction and Fantasy Writers of America Scholarships	**Varies**

Special Circumstances Scholarships

Scholarship	Deadline
Gates Millennium Scholars Program	**January**
Ronald McDonald House Charities Scholarships	**January**
Point Foundation Scholarships	**January**
Jackie Robinson Foundation Scholarship	**February 1**
Dream.US Opportunity Scholarship	**February**
National Garden Clubs Scholarships	**February**

Scholarship	Deadline
National Federation of State Poetry Societies Scholarships	**February**
National Beekeepers Association Scholarships	**Spring**
Foster Care to Success Scholarship	**March**
Casey Family Scholars Program	**Varies**
Orphan Foundation of America Scholarships	**March**
National Scrabble Association Scholarships	**Varies**
American Contract Bridge League Youth Scholarships	**May**
National Foster Parent Association Youth Scholarships	**March**
National Yo-Yo Association Scholarships	**Varies**
Jack Kent Cooke Foundation College Scholarship	**November**
Horatio Alger National Scholarship	**October**
Horatio Alger Targeted Programs	**State-specific deadlines**
Horatio Alger State Programs	**October**
Horatio Alger Military Family Scholarships	**Spring**
Horatio Alger Rural Students Scholarships	**October**
Horatio Alger Urban Students Scholarships	**October**
Horatio Alger CTE Programs	**Rolling basis**
Horatio Alger Scholars Conference Awards	**By invitation**
Horatio Alger Bridge to Success Scholarships	**Varies**
Horatio Alger Leadership in Adversity Awards	**October**
Horatio Alger Family Adversity Scholarships	**October**
Horatio Alger Academic Perseverance Awards	**October**
Horatio Alger Community Resilience Scholarships	**Varies**
Horatio Alger Courageous Leader Scholarships	**October**
Horatio Alger Survivors of Natural Disasters Scholarships	**Varies**
Horatio Alger Fire Survivors Scholarships	**Varies**
Horatio Alger Hurricane Survivors Scholarships	**Varies**
Horatio Alger Earthquake Survivors Scholarships	**Varies**
Horatio Alger Tornado Survivors Scholarships	**Varies**
Horatio Alger Flood Survivors Scholarships	**Varies**
Horatio Alger War-Impacted Students Scholarships	**Varies**
Horatio Alger Refugee Student Scholarships	**Varies**
Horatio Alger Rural Adversity Scholarships	**October**
Horatio Alger Urban Hardship Scholarships	**October**
Horatio Alger Special Medical Circumstances Scholarships	**Varies**

Scholarship	Deadline
Horatio Alger Family Caregiver Scholarships	**October**
Horatio Alger Traumatic Event Survivor Scholarships	**Varies**
Horatio Alger Loss of Parent Scholarships	**October**
Horatio Alger Homeless Students Scholarships	**Varies**
Horatio Alger Formerly Incarcerated Family Scholarships	**Varies**
Horatio Alger Immigrant Family Hardship Scholarships	**October**
Dell Scholars Program	**October**
Cameron Impact Scholarship	**September**
Shawn Carter Foundation Scholarship	**April**
Michael & Susan Dell Foundation Scholars Program	**December**
Posse Foundation Program	**Varies**
Horatio Alger Perseverance Awards	**October**
Gold Star Family Scholarship Fund	**Varies**
Children of Fallen Patriots Foundation Scholarships	**Rolling**
Families of Freedom Scholarship Fund	**Rolling**
Twin Towers Orphan Fund Scholarship	**Rolling**
Patriot Day Scholarship Program	**September**
Horatio Alger Courage Awards	**October**

Low-Income & First-Gen Access Scholarships

Scholarship	Deadline
Gates Millennium Scholars Program	**January**
Ronald McDonald House Charities Scholarships	**January**
Point Foundation Scholarships	**January**
Jackie Robinson Foundation Scholarship	**February 1**
Dream.US Opportunity Scholarship	**February**
National Garden Clubs Scholarships	**February**
National Federation of State Poetry Societies Scholarships	**February**
National Beekeepers Association Scholarships	**Spring**
Foster Care to Success Scholarship	**March**
Casey Family Scholars Program	**Varies**
Orphan Foundation of America Scholarships	**March**
National Scrabble Association Scholarships	**Varies**
American Contract Bridge League Youth Scholarships	**May**
National Foster Parent Association Youth Scholarships	**March**

Scholarship	Deadline
National Yo-Yo Association Scholarships	**Varies**
Jack Kent Cooke Foundation College Scholarship	**November**
Horatio Alger National Scholarship	**October**
Horatio Alger Targeted Programs	**State-specific deadlines**
Horatio Alger State Programs	**October**
Horatio Alger Military Family Scholarships	**Spring**
Horatio Alger Rural Students Scholarships	**October**
Horatio Alger Urban Students Scholarships	**October**
Horatio Alger CTE Programs	**Rolling basis**
Horatio Alger Scholars Conference Awards	**By invitation**
Horatio Alger Bridge to Success Scholarships	**Varies**
Horatio Alger Leadership in Adversity Awards	**October**
Horatio Alger Family Adversity Scholarships	**October**
Horatio Alger Academic Perseverance Awards	**October**
Horatio Alger Community Resilience Scholarships	**Varies**
Horatio Alger Courageous Leader Scholarships	**October**
Horatio Alger Survivors of Natural Disasters Scholarships	**Varies**
Horatio Alger Fire Survivors Scholarships	**Varies**
Horatio Alger Hurricane Survivors Scholarships	**Varies**
Horatio Alger Earthquake Survivors Scholarships	**Varies**
Horatio Alger Tornado Survivors Scholarships	**Varies**
Horatio Alger Flood Survivors Scholarships	**Varies**
Horatio Alger War-Impacted Students Scholarships	**Varies**
Horatio Alger Refugee Student Scholarships	**Varies**
Horatio Alger Rural Adversity Scholarships	**October**
Horatio Alger Urban Hardship Scholarships	**October**
Horatio Alger Special Medical Circumstances Scholarships	**Varies**
Horatio Alger Family Caregiver Scholarships	**October**
Horatio Alger Traumatic Event Survivor Scholarships	**Varies**
Horatio Alger Loss of Parent Scholarships	**October**
Horatio Alger Homeless Students Scholarships	**Varies**
Horatio Alger Formerly Incarcerated Family Scholarships	**Varies**
Horatio Alger Immigrant Family Hardship Scholarships	**October**

Scholarship	Deadline
Dell Scholars Program	**October**
Cameron Impact Scholarship	**September**
Shawn Carter Foundation Scholarship	**April**
Michael & Susan Dell Foundation Scholars Program	**December**
Posse Foundation Program	**Varies**
Horatio Alger Perseverance Awards	**October**
Gold Star Family Scholarship Fund	**Varies**
Children of Fallen Patriots Foundation Scholarships	**Rolling**
Families of Freedom Scholarship Fund	**Rolling**
Twin Towers Orphan Fund Scholarship	**Rolling**
Patriot Day Scholarship Program	**September**
Horatio Alger Courage Awards	**October**

Northeast Region Scholarships

State	Scholarship	Deadline
Illinois	Illinois Minority Teachers of Illinois Scholarship	**March 1**
Illinois	Illinois Golden Apple Scholars Program	**February**
Missouri	Access Missouri Financial Assistance Program	**February 1**
Wisconsin	Wisconsin Academic Excellence Scholarship	**February**
Michigan	Michigan Competitive Scholarship	**Annually**
Ohio	Ohio College Opportunity Grant	**October 1**
Indiana	Frank O'Bannon Grant (IN)	**April 15**
Ohio	Ohio War Orphans & Severely Disabled Veterans Scholarship	**July 1**
Ohio	Choose Ohio First Scholarship	**Varies by institution**
Ohio	Ohio STEM Scholarship	**Annually**
Indiana	21st Century Scholars Program (IN)	**June 30 of 8th grade year**
Missouri	Missouri Minority Teaching Scholarship	**June 1**
Minnesota	Minnesota Indian Scholarship Program	**July 1**
Iowa	Iowa Tuition Grant	**July 1**
Iowa	Iowa Vocational-Technical Grant	**July 1**
Iowa	Iowa Minority Academic Grant Aid Program	**July 1**
Iowa	Iowa Last-Dollar Scholarship	**July 1**
Minnesota	Minnesota GI Bill Scholarship	**Rolling**

State	Scholarship	Deadline
Minnesota	Minnesota State Grant	**Annually**
Minnesota	Minnesota Achieve Scholarship	**Annually**
South Dakota	South Dakota Opportunity Scholarship	**September 1**
South Dakota	South Dakota Freedom Scholarship	**Annually**
Wisconsin	Wisconsin Grant	**Annually**
Wisconsin	Wisconsin Talent Incentive Program Grant	**Annually**
Wisconsin	Wisconsin Minority Undergraduate Retention Grant	**Annually**
North Dakota	North Dakota State Grant	**Annually**
North Dakota	North Dakota Scholars Program	**Annually**
Missouri	A+ Scholarship Program (MO)	**Annually**
Missouri	Missouri Bright Flight Program	**August 1**
Illinois	Illinois Monetary Award Program (MAP)	**Annually, based on FAFSA submission date**
Illinois	Chicago STAR Scholarship	**Annually**
Illinois	CPS Scholarship Program	**Annually**
Indiana	Mitch Daniels Early Graduation Scholarship (IN)	**Annually**
Indiana	Indiana Nursing Scholarship Fund	**Annually**
Illinois	Illinois Special Education Teacher Scholarship	**Annually**
Illinois	Horatio Alger First-Generation Scholarships	**October**
Illinois	Horatio Alger State Programs	**October**
Illinois	Horatio Alger Rural Students Scholarships	**October**
Illinois	Horatio Alger Urban Students Scholarships	**October**
Illinois	Horatio Alger CTE Programs	**Rolling basis**
Illinois	Horatio Alger Military Family Scholarships	**Spring**
Illinois	Horatio Alger Targeted Programs	**State-specific deadlines**
Illinois	Horatio Alger Bridge to Success Scholarships	**Varies**
Illinois	Horatio Alger Leadership in Adversity Awards	**October**
Illinois	Horatio Alger Family Adversity Scholarships	**October**
Illinois	Horatio Alger Academic Perseverance Awards	**October**

State	Scholarship	Deadline
Illinois	Horatio Alger Community Resilience Scholarships	**Varies**
Illinois	Horatio Alger Courageous Leader Scholarships	**October**

South Region Scholarships

State	Scholarship	Deadline (2026)
Mississippi	Mississippi Eminent Scholars Grant	March 31 annually
Mississippi	HELP (Higher Education Legislative Plan for Needy Students)	March 31 annually
Mississippi	Nissan Scholarship Program (MS)	March 31 annually
Mississippi	Mississippi Teacher Loan/Scholarship Program	March 31 annually
Alabama	Alabama Teachers in Training Scholarship	March 1 annually
Alabama	Alabama Student Grant Program	Varies by institution
Alabama	CollegeCounts Scholarship (AL)	February 27 annually
Alabama	Alabama Student Assistance Program	As soon as possible after October 1 annually
Alabama	Alabama G.I. Dependents Scholarship Program	Rolling
Tennessee	Tennessee HOPE Scholarship	September 1 or February 1 annually
Tennessee	Tennessee Promise Scholarship	November 1 annually
Tennessee	Tennessee ASPIRE Award	September 1 or February 1 annually
Tennessee	Wilder-Naifeh Technical Skills Grant	Varies by institution
Tennessee	Tennessee Ned McWherter Scholars Program	February 15 annually
Texas	Texas Grant (TEXAS Grant)	January 15 annually
Texas	Texas Educational Opportunity Grant	January 15 annually
Texas	Top 10% Scholarship Program (TX)	January 15 annually
Texas	Terry Foundation Scholarship (TX)	Varies by institution
Texas	Houston Livestock Show and Rodeo Scholarship (TX)	February 1 annually
Louisiana	Louisiana State University Flagship Scholars	November 15 priority

State	Scholarship	Deadline (2026)
Louisiana	Rockefeller State Wildlife Scholarship	July 1 annually
Louisiana	Taylor Opportunity Program for Students (TOPS)	July 1 annually
Louisiana	Louisiana GO Grant	FAFSA priority date
Florida	Florida Bright Futures Scholarship Program	August 31 annually
Florida	José Martí Scholarship Challenge Grant Fund (FL)	April 1 annually
Florida	Florida Student Assistance Grant	Varies by institution
Florida	Florida Resident Access Grant	Varies by institution
Florida	Florida Tuition Aid Grant	Varies by institution
South Carolina	Palmetto Fellows Scholarship (SC)	April 15 early, June 15 final
South Carolina	LIFE Scholarship (SC)	Varies by institution
South Carolina	HOPE Scholarship (SC)	Varies by institution
South Carolina	South Carolina Tuition Grants	June 30 annually
South Carolina	SC Teaching Fellows Program	December 1 annually
Georgia	HOPE Scholarship (GA)	Varies by institution
Georgia	Zell Miller Scholarship (GA)	Varies by institution
Georgia	Georgia Tuition Equalization Grant	Varies by institution
Georgia	REACH Georgia Scholarship	Determined by school district
Georgia	Georgia Governor's Scholarship	Determined by local school systems
Virginia	Virginia Guaranteed Assistance Program	March 1 annually
Virginia	Virginia College Scholarship Assistance Program	March 1 annually
Virginia	Virginia Brown v. Board of Education Scholarship	March 1 annually
Virginia	Virginia Teaching Scholarship Loan Program	May 1 annually
Virginia	Virginia Tuition Assistance Grant	July 31 annually

West Region Scholarships

State	Scholarship	Deadline (2026)
California	California Teachers Association Scholarships	**January 31 annually**
Arizona	Arizona State University President's Scholarship	**January 15 annually**
California	California Dream Act Cal Grants	**March 2 annually**
California	Middle Class Scholarship (CA)	**March 2 annually**
California	Cal Grant Program	**March 2 annually**
California	California Wine Grape Growers Foundation Scholarships	**March 1 annually**
California	California Strawberry Scholarship Fund	**February 15 annually**
California	San Diego Foundation Scholarships	**February 2 annually**
California	California PTA Scholarships	**February 1 annually**
California	Hispanic Association of Colleges and Universities (CA regional branch)	**Varies by program**
Oregon	Oregon Promise Scholarship	**June 1 annually**
Oregon	Oregon Opportunity Grant	**Apply as soon as possible after October 1**
Oregon	Ford Family Foundation Scholarship (OR)	**March 1 annually**
Oregon	Oregon Barber & Hairdresser Scholarship	**March 1 annually**
Oregon	Oregon Tribal Student Scholarship	**March 1 annually**
Washington	Washington Opportunity Scholarship	**February 6 annually**
Washington	Washington College Grant	**Varies by institution**
Washington	College Bound Scholarship (WA)	**June 30 of 8th grade year to sign up**
Nevada	Millennium Scholarship (NV)	**Automatically awarded if eligible**
Nevada	Nevada Silver State Opportunity Grant	**Priority given to early FAFSA applicants**
Nevada	Nevada Women's Fund Scholarships	**February 28 annually**
Nevada	Truckee Meadows Community College Scholarships	**March 1 annually**
Nevada	College of Southern Nevada Foundation Scholarships	**March 1 annually**

State	Scholarship	Deadline (2026)
Colorado	Colorado Garden Foundation Scholarships	**March 15 annually**
Colorado	Colorado College Opportunity Fund	**Varies by institution**
Colorado	Denver Scholarship Foundation	**May 1 annually**
Colorado	Boettcher Foundation Scholarship (CO)	**November 1 annually**
Colorado	Daniels Fund Scholarship (CO)	**October 15 annually**
Utah	Utah Promise Scholarship	**FAFSA priority date**
Utah	Utah Opportunity Scholarship	**February 1 annually**
Utah	T.H. Bell Teaching Incentive Loan Program (UT)	**March 1 annually**
Utah	Regents' Scholarship (UT)	**February 1 annually**
Utah	Utah New Century Scholarship	**February 1 annually**
Arizona	Arizona Leveraging Educational Assistance Partnership	**FAFSA priority date**
Arizona	Northern Arizona University Lumberjack Scholars Award	**November 15 priority date**
Arizona	University of Arizona Wildcat Excellence Scholarship	**May 1 annually**

Pacific & Territories Scholarships

Here is the **chronologically ordered list** of **state-based scholarships** for **Hawaii, Alaska, and U.S. Territories**:

State/Territory	Scholarship	Deadline (2026)
Hawaii	University of Hawaii Regents and Presidential Scholarships	**January 15 annually**
Alaska	Alaska Space Grant Program	**February 1 annually**
Hawaii	Native Hawaiian Health Scholarship Program	**March 15 annually**
Hawaii	Hawaii B Plus Scholarship	**March 1 annually**
Hawaii	Hawaii Opportunity Grant	**March 1 annually**
Alaska	Alaska Performance Scholarship	**FAFSA priority deadline June 30 annually**
Alaska	Alaska Education Grant	**FAFSA submission by June 30 annually**

State/Territory	Scholarship	Deadline (2026)
Hawaii	Hawaii State Tuition Waiver Program	**Varies by institution**
Guam	Guam Territorial Scholarship	**April 30 annually**
American Samoa	American Samoa Government Scholarship	**April 30 annually**
Virgin Islands	Virgin Islands Territorial Scholarship	**April 30 annually**
Northern Mariana Islands	Northern Mariana Islands Scholarship Grant	**May 31 annually**
Puerto Rico	Puerto Rico Government Scholarship Program	**Varies annually**
Alaska	University of Alaska Scholars Program	**Automatically awarded based on high school ranking**
Alaska	Alaska Native Tribal Health Consortium Scholarships	**Varies annually**

Nationally Competitive & Prestigious Scholarships

Scholarship	Deadline
Goldwater Scholarship	**Late January**
Boren Scholarship	**Early February**
Truman Scholarship	**Early February**
Critical Language Scholarship (CLS)	**November**
Soros Fellowship for New Americans	**Late October**
Rhodes Scholarship	**Early October**
Marshall Scholarship	**Late Sept/Early Oct**
Mitchell Scholarship	**Late September**
Fulbright U.S. Student Program	**October**
Pickering Foreign Affairs Fellowship	**Late September**
Payne International Development Fellowship	**November**
Schwarzman Scholars Program	**September (global), May (China)**
Obama Foundation Scholars Program	**December**
Knight-Hennessy Scholars Program	**October**
Churchill Scholarship	**Early November**
Davidson Fellows Scholarship	**February**

Scholarship	Deadline
Jack Kent Cooke Graduate Arts Award	**November**
Hertz Fellowship	**Late October**
NSF Graduate Research Fellowship	**October**
Ford Foundation Fellowship	**December**
Schwarzman Scholars Program	**September (global), May (China)**
Gates Cambridge Scholarship	**October or December**
Rangel International Affairs Program Scholarship	**Mid-September**
Mitchell Scholarship	**Late September**

Military Related Scholarships

Scholarship	Deadline
Army ROTC Scholarship	**January 10 annually**
Army Women's Foundation Legacy Scholarship	**January 20 annually**
Navy ROTC Scholarship	**December 31 annually**
Air Force ROTC Scholarship	**December 31 annually**
Marine Corps ROTC Scholarship	**January 31 annually**
Coast Guard College Student Pre-Commissioning Initiative Scholarship	**Varies by recruiting office**
Army Health Professions Scholarship Program	**Rolling**
Navy Health Professions Scholarship Program	**Rolling**
Air Force Health Professions Scholarship Program	**Rolling**
Military Spouse Career Advancement Account Scholarship (MyCAA)	**Rolling**
Fisher House Foundation Scholarships for Military Children	**February 14 annually**
ThanksUSA Military Family Scholarship	**May 15 annually**
Freedom Alliance Scholarship Fund	**Rolling**
Military Officers Association of America (MOAA) Scholarship	**March 1 annually**
Pat Tillman Foundation Scholarship	**February 1 annually**
Navy-Marine Corps Relief Society Scholarships	**May 15 annually**
Air Force Aid Society Education Support Scholarships	**April 30 annually**
Marine Corps Scholarship Foundation	**March 1 annually**
Folds of Honor Foundation Scholarships	**March 31 annually**

Scholarship	Deadline
American Legion Legacy Scholarship	**April 1 annually**
Army Emergency Relief Scholarships	**April 1 annually**
AMVETS National Scholarship Program	**May 1 annually**
Paralyzed Veterans of America Scholarship	**June 30 annually**
VFW Voice of Democracy Scholarship	**October 31 annually**
VFW Patriot's Pen Scholarship	**October 31 annually**
Disabled American Veterans (DAV) Charitable Service Trust Scholarships	**Varies annually**
Iraq and Afghanistan Service Grant	**FAFSA priority deadlines**
Survivors' and Dependents' Educational Assistance Program (DEA)	**Rolling**
Children of Fallen Patriots Foundation Scholarships	**Rolling**
Tragedy Assistance Program for Survivors (TAPS) Scholarships	**Varies annually**
Marine Corps League Scholarships	**April 1 annually**
Navy League of the United States Scholarships	**March 1 annually**
Coast Guard Foundation Scholarships	**March 15 annually**
Army Women's Foundation Legacy Scholarship	**January 20 annually**
Armed Forces Communications & Electronics Association (AFCEA) Scholarships	**May 31 annually**
Association of the United States Army (AUSA) Scholarships	**July 1 annually**
Air Force Sergeants Association Scholarships	**March 31 annually**
Enlisted Association of the National Guard Scholarships	**May 1 annually**
Non-Commissioned Officers Association Scholarships	**March 31 annually**
Military Family Support Trust Scholarships	**February 1 annually**
National Military Family Association Scholarships	**Varies annually**

Ethnicity & Race Scholarships

Scholarship	Deadline (2026)
Ron Brown Scholar Program	**January**
Jackie Robinson Foundation Scholarship	**January**
National Society of Black Engineers Scholarships	**January**
HSF Gates Millennium Scholars Program	**January**

Scholarship	Deadline (2026)
Asian & Pacific Islander American Scholarship Fund (APIASF)	**January**
APIA General Scholarship Program	**January**
Kosciuszko Foundation Scholarships (Polish American)	**January**
United Negro College Fund (UNCF) General Scholarships	**Varies by program**
UNCF Scholars Program	**Varies annually**
Thurgood Marshall College Fund Scholarships	**Varies**
National Association for the Advancement of Colored People (NAACP) Scholarships	**Varies**
National Urban League Scholarships	**Varies**
Congressional Black Caucus Foundation Scholarships	**Varies**
National Black MBA Association Scholarships	**Varies**
National Association of Black Accountants Scholarships	**Varies annually**
National Black Nurses Association Scholarships	**March**
Hispanic Scholarship Fund (HSF) General Scholarships	**February**
HSF STEM Scholarships	**February**
Hispanic Association of Colleges and Universities Scholarships	**Varies annually**
Prospanica Foundation Scholarships	**April**
Society of Hispanic Professional Engineers (SHPE) Scholarships	**April**
National Association of Hispanic Nurses Scholarships	**April**
National Association of Hispanic Journalists Scholarships	**April**
Hispanic Dental Association Scholarships	**Varies annually**
Hispanic Scholarship Fund	**Varies**
American Indian College Fund Scholarships	**May**
American Indian Higher Education Consortium Scholarships	**Varies**
American Indian Graduate Center Scholarships	**Varies**
Cobell Scholarship Program (Native American)	**March**
Catching the Dream Scholarship (Native American)	**March**
Native Forward Scholars Fund	**Varies**
National Indian Education Association Scholarships	**Varies annually**
Indian Health Service Scholarship Program (Native American)	**February**
Association on American Indian Affairs Scholarships	**Varies**

Scholarship	Deadline (2026)
American Indian Science and Engineering Society (AISES) Scholarships	**May**
Bureau of Indian Education Higher Education Grant Program	**Varies annually**
Alaska Native Science & Engineering Program Scholarships	**Varies**
Sealaska Heritage Scholarships (Alaska Native)	**March**
Native Hawaiian Education Scholarship Program	**April**
Native Hawaiian Health Scholarship Program	**Varies annually**
Native Hawaiian Chamber of Commerce Scholarships	**April**
Arab American Institute Scholarships	**Varies**
American-Arab Anti-Discrimination Committee Scholarships	**Varies annually**
American Druze Foundation Scholarships	**May**
Turkish American Scholarship Fund	**Varies annually**
National Italian American Foundation Scholarships	**March**
Order Sons and Daughters of Italy in America Scholarships	**February**
Columbus Citizens Foundation Scholarship	**February**
Italian Catholic Federation Scholarships	**March**
American Irish Historical Society Scholarships	**Varies annually**
Irish American Scholars Program	**February**
Ancient Order of Hibernians Scholarship	**Varies annually**
German American Heritage Foundation Scholarships	**May**
French-American Chamber of Commerce Scholarships	**Varies annually**
Polish American Congress Scholarships	**March**
American Hungarian Foundation Scholarships	**April**
Scandinavian American Foundation Scholarships	**March**
Norwegian-American Foundation Scholarships	**February**
Swedish Council of America Scholarships	**March**
Finnish-American Scholarship Program	**Varies annually**
Armenian General Benevolent Union Scholarships	**April**
Agnes Missirian Scholarship	**April**
ARS Undergraduate Scholarship	**March**
ASA Scholarships	**April**
Diocese of the Armenian Church of America (Eastern) Scholarships	**May**

Scholarship	Deadline (2026)
Helen C. Evans Scholarship	**April**

Religion Scholarships

Scholarship	Deadline
Baptist Joint Committee for Religious Liberty Scholarships	**Varies annually**
Baptist Leadership Scholars Program	**Varies by institution**
Southern Baptist Convention Seminary Scholarships	**Varies by seminary**
United Methodist Church General Board of Higher Education Scholarships	**March 1**
Disciples of Christ Higher Education & Leadership Ministries Scholarships	**March 15**
Lutheran Church Missouri Synod Scholarships	**March 1**
Evangelical Lutheran Church in America Fund for Leaders Scholarships	**February 15**
Presbyterian Church USA Scholarship Program	**May 1**
Presbyterian Church National Student Fund	**June 1**
Reformed Church in America Scholarships	**April 1**
Episcopal Church General Convention Scholarships	**May 1**
Anglican Communion Scholarship Fund	**April 15**
Catholic Knights of Columbus Scholarships	**March 1**
Catholic Daughters of the Americas Scholarships	**March 15**
Catholic Order of Foresters Scholarships	**April 30**
Catholic United Financial Scholarships	**February 15**
Catholic Youth Organization Scholarships	**March 31**
Catholic Daughters National College Scholarship	**March 15**
Catholic War Veterans Scholarships	**May 1**
National Catholic College Admission Association Scholarships	**March 1**
Jesuit Volunteer Corps Scholarships	**Varies**
Benedictine Scholarship Program	**March 15**
Franciscan Brothers Scholarship Program	**April 1**
Dominican Sisters College Scholarship Fund	**March 31**
Augustinian Student Scholars Program	**April 1**
Marianist Educational Foundation Scholarships	**March 31**
Jewish War Veterans Religious Scholarship	**April 15**

Scholarship	Deadline
Jewish Community Federation Scholarships	**March 15**
Jewish Theological Seminary Scholarships	**March 1**
Yeshiva University Merit Scholarships	**January 31**
Orthodox Union Scholarships	**April 1**
Hillel International Scholarships	**February 15**
Hebrew Free Loan Association Scholarships	**March 1**
Islamic Society of North America Scholarships	**May 1**
Islamic Scholarship Fund	**March 21**
Muslim Students Association National Scholarships	**March 15**
Muslim Youth of North America Scholarship Program	**April 15**
Islamic Relief USA Scholarships	**April 1**
Nation of Islam Scholarship Fund	**Varies**
Sikh American Legal Defense and Education Fund Scholarships	**April 15**
Sikh Foundation Scholarships	**March 31**
Sikh Coalition Scholarships	**April 30**
Hindu American Foundation Scholarships	**March 15**
Vishwa Hindu Parishad of America Scholarships	**April 1**
Jain Society of North America Scholarships	**March 31**
Buddhist Churches of America Scholarships	**April 15**
Buddhist Study Center Scholarships	**March 15**
Soka Gakkai International-USA Youth Scholarships	**April 1**
World Buddhist Association Scholarships	**Varies**
Christian Science Church Scholarships	**May 1**
Allan Jerome Burry Scholarship	**March 15**
Catholic United Financial College Tuition Scholarship	**February 15**
CCA Christian Cheer Nationals Scholarship	**December 31**
Champions for Christ Scholarship	**March 1**
Diller Teen Tikkun Olam Awards	**January 5**
Baptist Foundation of Illinois Scholarship Program	**March 31**
Emmett J. Doerr Memorial Scout Scholarship	**March 31**
Fadel Educational Foundation Annual Award Program	**April 30**
Helen B. and Lewis E. Goldstein Scholarship Fund	**March 1**
ISF Policy Scholarship Program	**March 21**
Islamic Society of North America Scholarships	**May 1**
Moris J. and Betty Kaplun Essay Contest	**March 15**

Scholarship	Deadline
National Presbyterian College Scholarship	**May 15**
Native American Education Grant (Presbyterian Church USA)	**June 1**
Opportunity Scholarships for Lutheran Laywomen	**April 15**
Otto M. Stanfield Legal Scholarship	**March 31**
Presbyterian Church USA Student Opportunity Scholarships	**May 15**
Rev. Dr. Karen Layman Gift of Hope Scholarship	**March 15**
Stanfield and D'Orlando Art Scholarship	**March 31**
Interfaith Youth Core – Interfaith Leadership Institute Awards	**April 15**
UCC Seminarian Scholarship	**April 1**
Undergraduate Scholarships (United Church of Christ)	**April 15**
United Methodist General Scholarship	**March 1**
Women in United Methodist History Writing Award	**March 15**
Young Christian Leaders Scholarship	**April 1**
Interfaith Youth Core Scholarships	**Varies each year**
Interfaith Alliance Foundation Scholarships	**March 15**
National Conference for Community and Justice Interfaith Scholarships	**April 30**
Parliament of the World's Religions Scholarships	**January 31**
United Religions Initiative Scholarships	**May 1**
American Academy of Religion Interfaith Scholarships	**March 1**
Council for a Parliament of World Religions Scholars Program	**February 15**
Interfaith America Student Fellowship Scholarships	**October 1**
BJC Fellows Program – Baptist Joint Committee for Religious Liberty	**April 1**
Pluralism Project Scholarships	**April 15**
Interfaith Peace Chapel Scholarship Fund	**May 15**
World Council of Churches Interfaith Scholarships	**March 31**
Ecumenical Women at the United Nations Scholarships	**January 15**
Temple of Understanding Interfaith Fellowship	**February 20**
Spiritual Directors International Scholarships	**June 1**
Universal Life Church Student Scholarship	**June 30**
Bahá'í Faith National Scholarship Fund	**March 1**
Bahá'í Service Corps Scholarships	**April 30**

Scholarship	Deadline
Bahá'í World Centre Fellowship	**January 15**
Zoroastrian Association of North America Scholarships	**May 1**
Zoroastrian Trust Funds of Europe Scholarships (U.S. students eligible)	**March 15**
Covenant of the Goddess Youth Scholarship	**May 31**
Covenant of Unitarian Universalist Pagans (CUUPS) Support Program	**Rolling**
Ancient Order of Druids in America Study Support	**March 1**
Japan Foundation Fellowship for Japanese Studies	**January 31**
Unitarian Universalist Association Scholarships	**March 1**
Universalist Heritage Foundation Scholarships	**April 15**
Quaker Friends General Conference Scholarships	**February 28**
Quaker United Nations Office Fellowship	**January 10**
Mennonite Church USA Scholarship Program	**March 31**
Mennonite Education Agency Scholarships	**April 15**
Moravian Church in America Scholarships	**March 1**
Shinto Foundation International Scholarship (U.S. eligible)	**January 31**
American Indian College Fund Tribal Scholarships	**May 31**
Native American Church of North America Scholarships	**March 31**
Yoruba Studies Association Research Fellowship	**May 15**
NALAC Afro-Latinx Scholarship Fund	**March 31**
CAPES Afro-Brazilian Cultural Research Fellowship	**July 1**
Haitian Studies Association Emerging Scholars Fellowship	**June 15**
Eckankar Spiritual Student Scholarship	**March 15**
Theosophical Society in America Scholarships	**May 1**
Anthroposophical Society Student Scholarship	**April 10**
Edgar Cayce A.R.E. Spiritual Study Scholarship	**August 1**
Hefferlin Foundation Ministerial Education Scholarships	**Rolling**
Religious Science International Scholarships	**June 15**
Ethical Culture Society Scholarships	**March 20**
Secular Student Alliance Interfaith Scholarships	**April 1**
Interfaith Social Action Student Scholarship	**May 31**
Multi-Faith Campus Alliance Scholarships	**June 15**
Spiritual Humanist Scholarship Program	**July 1**
KAICIID International Fellows Programme	**February 1**

Interfaith & Minor Religions

Scholarship	Deadline
Interfaith Youth Core Scholarships	**Varies each year**
Interfaith Alliance Foundation Scholarships	**March 15**
National Conference for Community and Justice Interfaith Scholarships	**April 30**
Parliament of the World's Religions Scholarships	**January 31**
United Religions Initiative Scholarships	**May 1**
American Academy of Religion Interfaith Scholarships	**March 1**
Council for a Parliament of World Religions Scholars Program	**February 15**
Interfaith America Student Fellowship Scholarships	**October 1**
BJC Fellows Program – Baptist Joint Committee for Religious Liberty	**April 1**
Pluralism Project Scholarships	**April 15**
Interfaith Peace Chapel Scholarship Fund	**May 15**
World Council of Churches Interfaith Scholarships	**March 31**
Ecumenical Women at the United Nations Scholarships	**January 15**
Temple of Understanding Interfaith Fellowship	**February 20**
Spiritual Directors International Scholarships	**June 1**
Universal Life Church Student Scholarship	**June 30**
Bahá'í Faith National Scholarship Fund	**March 1**
Bahá'í Service Corps Scholarships	**April 30**
Bahá'í World Centre Fellowship	**January 15**
Zoroastrian Association of North America Scholarships	**May 1**
Zoroastrian Trust Funds of Europe Scholarships (U.S. students eligible)	**March 15**
Covenant of the Goddess Youth Scholarship	**May 31**
Covenant of Unitarian Universalist Pagans (CUUPS) Support Program	**Rolling**
Ancient Order of Druids in America Study Support	**March 1**
Japan Foundation Fellowship for Japanese Studies	**January 31**
Unitarian Universalist Association Scholarships	**March 1**
Universalist Heritage Foundation Scholarships	**April 15**
Quaker Friends General Conference Scholarships	**February 28**
Quaker United Nations Office Fellowship	**January 10**
Mennonite Church USA Scholarship Program	**March 31**

Scholarship	Deadline
Mennonite Education Agency Scholarships	**April 15**
Moravian Church in America Scholarships	**March 1**
Shinto Foundation International Scholarship (U.S. eligible)	**January 31**
American Indian College Fund Tribal Scholarships	**May 31**
Native American Church of North America Scholarships	**March 31**
Yoruba Studies Association Research Fellowship	**May 15**
NALAC Afro-Latinx Scholarship Fund	**March 31**
CAPES Afro-Brazilian Cultural Research Fellowship	**July 1**
Haitian Studies Association Emerging Scholars Fellowship	**June 15**
Eckankar Spiritual Student Scholarship	**March 15**
Theosophical Society in America Scholarships	**May 1**
Anthroposophical Society Student Scholarship	**April 10**
Edgar Cayce A.R.E. Spiritual Study Scholarship	**August 1**
Hefferlin Foundation Ministerial Education Scholarships	**Rolling**
Religious Science International Scholarships	**June 15**
Ethical Culture Society Scholarships	**March 20**
Secular Student Alliance Interfaith Scholarships	**April 1**
Interfaith Social Action Student Scholarship	**May 31**
Multi-Faith Campus Alliance Scholarships	**June 15**
Spiritual Humanist Scholarship Program	**July 1**
KAICIID International Fellows Programme	**February 1**

Disability Scholarships

Scholarship	Deadline (2026)
Anne Ford Scholarship Program	**January**
Baer Reintegration Scholarship	**January**
Bristol-Myers Squibb Scholarship for Cancer Survivors	**January**
Cancer for College Scholarships	**January**
American Association of People with Disabilities (AAPD) Scholarships	**Spring**
National Center for Learning Disabilities Scholarships	**Spring**
Learning Disabilities Association of America Scholarships	**Spring**
American Foundation for the Blind Scholarships	**Spring**
National Federation of the Blind Scholarships	**March**
American Council of the Blind Scholarships	**Mid-March**

Scholarship	Deadline (2026)
National Association of Blind Students Scholarships	**Spring**
Guide Dog Foundation Student Scholarship	**Spring**
Hadley Institute for the Blind and Visually Impaired Scholarships	**Spring**
Nancy J. Bloch Leadership & Advocacy Scholarships	**Early Summer**
Alexander Graham Bell Association for the Deaf and Hard of Hearing Scholarships	**Spring**
Hearing Loss Association of America Scholarships	**Spring**
Sertoma Hard of Hearing or Deaf Scholarships	**Spring**
National Technical Institute for the Deaf Scholarships	**Varies by program**
American Speech-Language-Hearing Association Disability Scholarships	**Spring**
Gallaudet University Scholarships (disability branch)	**Varies by program**
American Sign Language Teachers Association Scholarships	**Spring**
CEC Yes I Can Scholarships (Council for Exceptional Children)	**Spring**
Easterseals Foundation Scholarships	**Spring**
March of Dimes Scholarship Program	**Spring**
Cerebral Palsy Foundation Scholarships	**Spring**
United Cerebral Palsy Scholarships	**Spring**
Spina Bifida Association Scholarships	**Spring**
Muscular Dystrophy Association Scholarships	**Spring**
Multiple Sclerosis Foundation Scholarships	**Spring**
Multiple Sclerosis Association of America Scholarships	**Spring**
American Epilepsy Society Scholarships	**Spring**
Epilepsy Foundation Scholarships	**Spring**
American Diabetes Association Student Scholarships	**Spring**
Juvenile Diabetes Research Foundation Scholarships	**Spring**
American Heart Association Disability Scholarships	**Spring**
American Lung Association Scholarships	**Spring**
Asthma and Allergy Foundation of America Scholarships	**Spring**
American Cancer Society Survivors Scholarship	**Spring**
Cancer Survivors' Fund Scholarships	**Spring**
Leukemia & Lymphoma Society Scholarships	**Spring**
Susan G. Komen Foundation Scholarships (cancer survivors branch)	**Spring**

Scholarship	Deadline (2026)
National Brain Tumor Society Scholarships	**Spring**
Brain Injury Association of America Scholarships	**Spring**
American Stroke Association Scholarships	**Spring**
American Kidney Fund Scholarships	**Spring**
National Kidney Foundation Scholarships	**Spring**
American Liver Foundation Scholarships	**Spring**
Cystic Fibrosis Foundation Scholarships	**Spring**
Crohn's & Colitis Foundation Scholarships	**Spring**
National Psoriasis Foundation Scholarships	**Spring**
Lupus Foundation of America Scholarships	**Spring**
Sickle Cell Disease Association Scholarships	**Spring**
Hemophilia Federation of America Scholarships	**Spring**
National Hemophilia Foundation Scholarships	**Spring**
American Chronic Pain Association Scholarships	**Spring**
Migraine Research Foundation Scholarships	**Spring**
Tourette Association of America Scholarships	**Spring**
Autism Society of America Scholarships	**Spring**
Autism Speaks Postsecondary Scholarships	**Spring**
Organization for Autism Research Scholarships	**Spring**
National Down Syndrome Society Scholarships	**Spring**
Global Down Syndrome Foundation Scholarships	**Spring**
Fragile X Foundation Scholarships	**Spring**
Williams Syndrome Association Scholarships	**Spring**
Turner Syndrome Society Scholarships	**Spring**
Rare Diseases Foundation Student Scholarship	**Spring**
Genetic Disorders Alliance Scholarships	**Spring**
Dyslexia Foundation Scholarships	**Spring**
National Dyslexia Association Scholarships	**Spring**
ADHD Awareness Student Scholarship	**Spring**
Anxiety and Depression Association of America Scholarships	**Spring**
National Alliance on Mental Illness (NAMI) Scholarships	**Spring**
Depression and Bipolar Support Alliance Scholarships	**Spring**
Mental Health America Scholarships	**Spring**

Scholarship	Deadline (2026)
Schizophrenia & Related Disorders Alliance Scholarships	**Spring**
PTSD Foundation of America Scholarships	**Spring**
Suicide Prevention Lifeline Youth Scholarship	**Spring**
International OCD Foundation Scholarships	**Spring**
Substance Abuse and Mental Health Services Administration Scholarships	**Spring**
Recovering Students Scholarship Fund	**Spring**
Alcoholics Anonymous Students in Recovery Scholarship	**Spring**
Narcotics Anonymous Students in Recovery Scholarship	**Spring**
Al-Anon Family Group Student Scholarships	**Spring**
Learning Ally Dyslexia Scholarship Program	**Spring**
Eye to Eye National Mentoring Scholarships (LD)	**Spring**
National Tourette Syndrome Association Scholarships	**Spring**
National Council on Independent Living Scholarships	**Spring**
National Organization on Disability Scholarships	**Spring**
American Association on Intellectual and Developmental Disabilities Scholarships	**Spring**
Association of University Centers on Disabilities Scholarships	**Spring**
National Autism Association Scholarships	**Spring**
Christopher & Dana Reeve Foundation Scholarships	**Spring**
Paralyzed Veterans of America (student branch)	**Spring**
Amputee Coalition of America Scholarships	**Spring**
Limb Loss Resource Center Scholarships	**Spring**
International Dyslexia Association Scholarships	**Spring**
Lighthouse Guild Vision Scholarships	**Spring**
Vision Council Foundation Scholarships	**Spring**
American Printing House for the Blind Scholarships	**Spring**
Perkins School for the Blind Student Scholarships	**Spring**
National Deaf Children's Society (U.S. students eligible)	**Spring**
Council on Disability Awareness Scholarships	**Spring**
HEATH Resource Center Postsecondary Disability Scholarships	**Spring**
AbbVie Immunology Scholarship	**Spring**
Alyssa McCroskey Memorial Scholarship	**Spring**

Scholarship	Deadline (2026)
Duane Buckley Memorial Scholarship	**Spring**
Dyslexia/Auditory Processing Disorder Scholarship	**Spring**
Elizabeth Nash Foundation Scholarship Program	**April**
Eric Dostie Memorial College Scholarship	**March**
Fred Scheigert Scholarships	**March**
George H. Nofer Scholarship for Law and Public Policy	**April**
Graeme Clark Scholarship	**September**
Guthrie-Koch PKU Scholarship	**March**
Harry Alan Gregg Foundation Grants	**Rolling Basis**
Help America Hear Scholarship	**April**
HIV-Positive Scholarship	**Varies annually**
Incight Scholarship	**April**
Jaime Guttenberg All Abilities Scholarship	**April**
Kevin Child Scholarship	**April**
L.I.F.E. Scholarship	**March**
Lime Connect Pathways Scholarship for High School Seniors with Disabilities	**Spring**
Little People of America Scholarships	**April**
Marion Huber Learning Through Listening Awards	**January**
Mary P. Oenslanger Scholastic Achievement Awards	**February**
Michael A. Hunter Memorial Scholarship Fund	**April**
Mike Hylton Memorial Scholarship	**May**
Millie Brother Scholarship	**April**
Millie Gonzalez Memorial Scholarships	**Varies annually**
National Collegiate Cancer Foundation Scholarship	**May**
National Scholarship Competition for Disabled College Students	**Spring**
NFMC Hinda Honigman Award for the Blind	**March**
Optimist International Communications Contest	**Varies by Local Club**
P. Buckley Moss Endowed Scholarship	**March**
Paul and Ellen Ruckes Scholarship	**March**
RAREis Scholarship	**May**
Rudolph Dillman Memorial Scholarship	**March**
Salix Gastrointestinal Health Scholars Award	**May**

Membership & Professional Association Scholarships

Scholarship	Deadline (2026)
National Honor Society (NHS) Scholarship	**November–December**
National Beta Club Scholarship	**January**
Phi Theta Kappa Honor Society Scholarships	**Varies by scholarship cycle**
Phi Beta Kappa Society Scholarships	**Varies**
Golden Key International Honour Society Scholarships	**Varies throughout the year**
Order of the Arrow (Boy Scouts) Scholarships	**January**
Eagle Scout National Scholarships	**January**
Girl Scouts Gold Award Scholarship	**Varies by council**
Girl Scouts Juliette Gordon Low Scholarship	**Varies**
4-H Youth Development Program Scholarships	**Varies by state program**
FFA (Future Farmers of America) Scholarships	**January**
FCCLA (Family, Career and Community Leaders of America) Scholarships	**March**
DECA Student Organization Scholarships	**January**
HOSA (Health Occupations Students of America) Scholarships	**March**
SkillsUSA National Scholarships	**February**
BPA (Business Professionals of America) Scholarships	**March**
TSA (Technology Student Association) Scholarships	**March**
Junior Achievement Student Scholarships	**Varies by region**
Key Club International Scholarships	**February**
Kiwanis International Scholarships	**Varies by district**
Rotary Youth Leadership Awards Scholarships	**Varies by Rotary district**
Lions Club International Scholarships	**Varies by local club**
Optimist International Scholarships	**February**
Jaycees International Scholarships	**Varies**
Knights of Columbus Scholarships	**March**
Knights of Peter Claver Scholarships	**February**
Catholic Daughters of the Americas Scholarships	**March**
Sons of Italy Membership Scholarships	**February**
Daughters of Italy Membership Scholarships	**February**

Scholarship	Deadline (2026)
Ancient Order of Hibernians Membership Scholarships	**March**
Sons of the American Revolution Scholarships	**December or January**
Daughters of the American Revolution General Membership Scholarships	**January**
Colonial Dames of America Scholarships	**February**
Mayflower Society Scholarships	**March**
General Society of Colonial Wars Scholarships	**Varies by chapter**
Sons of Union Veterans of the Civil War Scholarships	**March**
United Daughters of the Confederacy Scholarships	**March**
Elks National Foundation Legacy Awards	**February**
Moose International Scholarships	**December**
Loyal Order of the Moose Heart of the Community Scholarship	**January**
Eagles (Fraternal Order of Eagles) Scholarship	**February**
Odd Fellows and Rebekahs Scholarships	**March**
Masonic Grand Lodge Scholarships	**Varies by lodge**
Order of the Eastern Star Scholarships	**February**
Shriners International Scholarships	**March**
Scottish Rite Foundation Scholarships	**March**
Job's Daughters International Scholarships	**March**
International Order of the Rainbow for Girls Scholarships	**March**
DeMolay International Scholarships	**March**
American Legion Auxiliary Scholarships	**March**
Sons of the American Legion Scholarships	**March**
Veterans of Foreign Wars Auxiliary Scholarships	**March**
AMVETS Auxiliary Scholarships	**March**
Disabled American Veterans Auxiliary Scholarships	**March**
Marine Corps League Auxiliary Scholarships	**March**
Navy League Auxiliary Scholarships	**March**
Daughters of the Nile Foundation Scholarships	**March**
National Panhellenic Conference Sorority Scholarships	**Varies by sorority**
North-American Interfraternity Conference Scholarships	**Varies by fraternity**
Alpha Phi Alpha Fraternity Scholarships	**February**

Scholarship	Deadline (2026)
Alpha Kappa Alpha Sorority Scholarships	**Varies by chapter and program cycle**
Kappa Alpha Psi Fraternity Scholarships	**April**
Omega Psi Phi Fraternity Scholarships	**April**
Delta Sigma Theta Sorority Scholarships	**February**
Phi Beta Sigma Fraternity Scholarships	**Varies by chapter**
Zeta Phi Beta Sorority Scholarships	**April**
Sigma Gamma Rho Sorority Scholarships	**Varies by chapter**
Iota Phi Theta Fraternity Scholarships	**March**
Lambda Theta Alpha Sorority Scholarships	**April**
Lambda Theta Phi Fraternity Scholarships	**April**
Sigma Lambda Beta Fraternity Scholarships	**April**
Sigma Lambda Gamma Sorority Scholarships	**Varies by chapter**
Phi Mu Sorority Scholarships	**March**
Sigma Chi Fraternity Scholarships	**February**
Kappa Kappa Gamma Sorority Scholarships	**March**
Gaston/Nolle Scholarships	**Varies by year**
Alpha Kappa Alpha Financial Need Scholars	**Varies by year**
Educational Advancement Foundation Merit Scholarship	**Varies each year**
Youth Partners Accessing Capital	**Spring each year**
Alpha Kappa Psi Scholarships	**Spring each year**
AAAE Foundation Scholarship	**Spring each year**
American Association of State Troopers Scholarship	**Spring each year**
ACJA Lambda Alpha Epsilon Scholarship	**Spring each year**
Student Paper Competition	**Spring each year**
American Culinary Federation Scholarships	**Spring and fall each year**
Ray and Gertrude Marshall Scholarship	**Spring each year**
ADHA Institute Scholarship Program	**February**
Colgate Bright Smiles Bright Futures Minority Scholarships	**February**
Crest Oral B Laboratories Dental Hygiene Scholarships	**February**
Dr. Esther Wilkins Scholarship	**February**
Irene Woodall Graduate Scholarship	**February**

Scholarship	Deadline (2026)
Karla Girts Memorial Community Outreach Scholarship	**February**
Sigma Phi Alpha Undergraduate Scholarship	**February**
AFSCME Family Scholarship	**December**
Robert G. Porter Post Secondary Scholarships	**Spring each year**
Robert G. Porter Scholars Program for Members	**Spring each year**
AFSA Financial Aid Scholarships	**February**
AHIMA Foundation Merit Scholarships	**September**
Charlotte McGuire Scholarship	**April**
Cedarcrest Farms Scholarship	**Varies by year**
American Legion Eagle Scout of the Year	**March**
Eight and Forty Lung and Respiratory Nursing Scholarship Fund	**May**
Children of Warriors National Presidents' Scholarship	**March**
Junior Member Loyalty Scholarship	**March**
Non Traditional Student Scholarship	**March**
Spirit of Youth Scholarship for Junior Members	**March**
American Legion Auxiliary Department of California Educational Assistance General 1,000 Dollar Scholarships	**March**
American Legion Auxiliary Department of California Educational Assistance General 2,000 Dollar Scholarships	**March**
American Legion Auxiliary Department of California Educational Assistance General 500 Dollar Scholarships	**March**
Past Department Presidents' Junior Scholarship Award	**March**
American Legion Department of Florida General Scholarship	**March**
Florida Oratorical Contest	**January**
Boy Scout and Eagle Scout Scholarship	**March**
Kappa Delta Phi	**Spring each year**
Mary Eileen Dixey Scholarship	**March**
Cedarcrest Farms Scholarship	**Varies by year**
American Legion Eagle Scout of the Year	**March**
Don Riebhoff Memorial Scholarship	**January**
Dr. James L. Lawson Memorial Scholarship	**January**
Edmond A. Metzger Scholarship	**January**

Scholarship	Deadline (2026)
Fred R. McDaniel Memorial Scholarship	January
Gary Wagner K3OMI Scholarship	January
IRARC Memorial Joseph P. Rubino WA4MMD Scholarship	January
Irving W. Cook WA0CGS Scholarship	January
K2TEO Martin J. Green Sr. Memorial Scholarship	January
L. Phil and Alice J. Wicker Scholarship	January
L. B. Cebik W4RNL and Jean Cebik N4TZP Memorial Scholarship	January
Louisiana Memorial Scholarship	January
Mary Lou Brown Scholarship	January
Mississippi Scholarship	January
New England FEMARA Scholarships	January
Paul and Helen L. Grauer Scholarship	January
PHD Scholarship	January
Ray N0RP and Katie W0KTE Pautz Scholarship	January
Richard W. Bendicksen N7ZL Memorial Scholarship	January
Six Meter Club of Chicago Scholarship	January
Tom and Judith Comstock Scholarship	January
YASME Foundation Scholarship	January
You've Got a Friend in Pennsylvania Scholarship	January
Samuel Fletcher Tapman ASCE Student Chapter Club Scholarship	February
Trent R. Dames and William W. Moore Fellowship	February
Mackinac Scholarship	Varies
Marvin L. Zuidema Scholarship Award	February
ASME Auxiliary Lucy and Charles W. E. Clarke Scholarship	February
Berna Lou Cartwright Scholarship	February
F. W. Beich Beichley Scholarship	February
Frank and Dorothy Miller ASME Auxiliary Scholarships	February
Garland Duncan Scholarships	February
International Gas Turbine Institute Scholarship	March
John and Elsa Gracik Scholarships	February
Kenneth Andrew Roe Scholarship	February

Scholarship	Deadline (2026)
Melvin R. Green Scholarships	February
Old Guard Oral Presentation Competition	Annual competition, spring
Elekta Radiation Therapy Scholarship	April
AMVETS National Scholarships for Entering College Freshman	April
AMVETS National Scholarships for Veterans	April
AMVETS National Ladies Auxiliary Scholarship	April
Angus Foundation Scholarships	May
Appaloosa Youth Association Art Contest	March
Appaloosa Youth Association Essay Contest	March
The Scholastic Art & Writing Awards	Varies (usually Dec-Jan)
Youth Program	Varies
ARA Scholarship	March
Petroleum Division College Scholarships	March
Women in Sports Media Scholarship Internship Program	January
Association of Flight Attendants Annual Scholarship	April
National Academic Scholarships	Varies
AORN Foundation Scholarship Program	June
Assured Life Association National Scholarship	March
David B. Durkee Memorial Scholarship Program	March
Big Y Scholarship Programs	February
Bob Warnicke Scholarship	March
Boys and Girls Clubs of America National Youth of the Year Award	Nominations
CTA César E. Chávez and Dolores Huerta Education Award Program	March
Martin Luther King Jr. Memorial Scholarship	February
Student CTA Scholarship in Honor of L. Gordon Bittle	March
Catholic United Financial College Tuition Scholarship	February
Kiwanis Children's Fund Scholarship	February
Dollars for Scholars Scholarship	Varies by local chapter
Shropshire Scholarship	March

Scholarship	Deadline (2026)
CWA Joe Beirne Foundation Scholarship	April
Conference of Minority Transportation Officials National Scholarship	May
CTAHPERD Gibson Laemel Scholarship	March
Mary Benevento CTAHPERD Scholarship	March
Stella Blum Research Grant	May
Harry A. Applegate Scholarship	March
Payzer Scholarship	March
Christopher L. Hunt Scholarship	April
Dr. Kenny D. Hasija Scholarship	April
Educational Theatre Association Board of Directors Scholarship	March
Educational Theatre Association Presidents Leadership Scholarship	March
Michael J. Peitz Leadership Scholarship	March
Emergency Educational Fund Grants	October
Capt. James J. Regan Scholarship	March
James E. Breining Scholarship Award	April
National Aviation Explorer Scholarships	April
Sheryl A. Horak Memorial Scholarship	March
Texas Association FCCLA Regional Scholarship	March
FEEA Scholarship Program	March
Fleet Reserve Association Scholarship	April
Fraternal Order of Eagles Memorial Foundation	May
General Society of Mayflower Descendants Scholarship	March

Sponsor-Specific Scholarships

Scholarship	Deadline
Coca-Cola Scholars Foundation Scholarship	**October**
PepsiCo Foundation Scholarship	**Varies**
Dr Pepper Tuition Giveaway Scholarship	**November**
Burger King Scholars Program	**December**
McDonald's HACER National Scholarship	**February**
Taco Bell Live Más Scholarship	**January**
Chick-fil-A Remarkable Futures Scholarship	**December**

Scholarship	Deadline
Starbucks College Achievement Plan Scholarships	**Varies**
Dunkin' Donuts Foundation Scholarship	**April**
Subway Fresh Start Scholarship	**March**
Domino's Partner Scholarship	**Varies**
Wendy's High School Heisman Scholarship	**October**
Kroger Scholars Program	**April**
Walmart Foundation Scholarships	**January**
Thurgood Marshall/Apple HBCU Scholars Program	**Varies**
Costco Scholars Program	**March**
Amazon Future Engineer Scholarship	**January**
Google Scholarship Programs	**Varies**
Microsoft Tuition Scholarship	**January**
Apple Scholars Program	**February**
Meta Elevate Scholarship	**Varies**
Intel Scholars Program	**March**
IBM Tech Re-Entry & Academic Initiative	**Varies**
Oracle Scholars Program	**March**
Cisco Global Scholars	**February**
Adobe Scholars Program	**March**
Dell Technologies Scholarships	**March**
HP Foundation Scholars	**April**
Qualcomm Scholars Fund	**February**
NVIDIA Scholars Program	**March**
Palantir Global Scholars Program	**April**
Salesforce Scholars Program	**February**
Lockheed Martin STEM Scholars	**April**
Boeing Scholars Program	**March**
Northrop Grumman Foundation Scholars	**April**
Raytheon Technologies Scholars	**March**
General Electric Foundation Scholars	**April**
Siemens Foundation Scholarships	**February**
ExxonMobil Scholars Program	**March**
Shell Oil Company Technical Scholarship	**March**
Chevron Scholars Fund	**February**
Phillips 66 Scholars Program	**February**
ConocoPhillips Scholars Program	**February**

Scholarship	Deadline
BP Global Scholars Program	March
Marathon Petroleum Scholars Program	March
Fluor Foundation Scholarships	February
Bechtel Corporation Scholars	March
Jacobs Engineering Foundation Scholarships	February
Kiewit Foundation Scholarships	March
Black & Veatch Scholars Program	February
Toyota Scholars Program	February
Ford Motor Company Scholars Program	March
General Motors Scholars Program	February
Honda Scholars Fund	March
Nissan North America Scholars Program	February
Hyundai Scholars Program	March
Kia Scholars Program	March
Volkswagen of America Scholars Program	April
BMW of North America Scholarship Fund	March
Mercedes-Benz USA Scholarships	February
Porsche North America Scholarship Fund	March
Audi USA Foundation Scholarships	March
Tesla Scholars Program	February
SpaceX Scholars Program	March
Blue Origin Scholars Program	March
Virgin Galactic Scholars Program	March
Delta Air Lines Foundation Scholarship	February
United Airlines Foundation Scholarship	March
American Airlines Education Foundation Scholarship	February
Southwest Airlines Scholars Program	March
FedEx Scholars Program	April
UPS Scholars Program	March
DHL Scholars Fund	April
CSX Transportation Scholars Program	March
Union Pacific Railroad Scholarship Fund	March
BNSF Railway Foundation Scholarships	April
Norfolk Southern Foundation Scholarships	March
American Express Scholars Program	March
Visa Scholars Program	April

Scholarship	Deadline
Mastercard Scholars Program	**March**
Discover Financial Services Scholarship	**February**
Capital One Scholars Program	**March**
Bank of America Scholars Fund	**February**
JPMorgan Chase & Co. Scholars Program	**March**
Wells Fargo Scholars Program	**February**
Citigroup Scholars Program	**March**
Goldman Sachs Scholars Program	**April**
Morgan Stanley Scholars Program	**March**
BlackRock Scholars Program	**February**
Fidelity Investments Scholars Program	**March**
Charles Schwab Scholars Program	**February**
Vanguard Scholars Fund	**March**
T. Rowe Price Scholars Program	**March**
State Farm Foundation Scholars	**February**
Allstate Foundation Scholarships	**February**
Progressive Insurance Scholars Program	**March**
Nationwide Insurance Scholars Fund	**March**
Travelers Insurance Foundation Scholarships	**February**
Liberty Mutual Foundation Scholarships	**March**
Prudential Financial Scholars Program	**February**

Women in STEM Scholarships

Scholarship	Deadline
Society of Women Engineers (SWE) Scholarships	**February**
Google Women Techmakers Scholarship	**December**
AnitaB.org Grace Hopper Celebration Scholarships	**March**
NCWIT Collegiate Award for Women in Computing	**November**
NCWIT Aspirations in Computing Award	**October**
Palantir Women in Technology Scholarship	**March**
Adobe Research Women-in-Technology Scholarship	**September**
Microsoft Women in STEM Scholarship	**January**
Apple WWDC Swift Student Challenge	**April**
Society of Women Engineers	**March**

Scholarship	Deadline
American Association of University Women	**November–December**
NCWIT Aspirations in Computing (AiC) Award	**November**
Adobe Women-in-Technology Scholarship	**November–December**
Dell Women in Engineering Scholarship	**March**
HP Women InNovemberators in STEM Scholarship	**March**
NVIDIA Women in AI Scholarship	**March**
Qualcomm Women Engineers Scholarship	**February**
Accenture Women in Tech Scholarship	**April**
Deloitte Women in Data Science Scholarship	**February**
PwC Women in Analytics Fellowship	**March**
Ernst & Young (EY) Women in STEM Program	**March**
KPMG Women in Technology Scholarship	**March**
Bain & Company Women in Tech Scholarship	**March**
McKinsey Women in Data & Digital Fellowship	**March**
Women in CyberSecurity (WiCyS) Student Scholarship	**January**
DEF CON Women in Security Scholarship	**March**
Black Hat Women in Cybersecurity Scholarship	**April**
RSA Conference Women in Cybersecurity Scholarship	**February**
AnitaB.org TechWomen Program	**November**
TechGirls U.S. Department of State Program	**January**
Microsoft DigiGirlz STEM Scholarship	**March**
Google Code with Girls Program Scholarship	**March**
Amazon Girls in STEM Scholars Fund	**March**
Apple Swift Girls Coding Scholarship	**April**
Intel She Will InNovemberate Scholarship	**February**
IBM Women in Quantum Computing Fellowship	**March**
NVIDIA Women in Deep Learning Scholarship	**March**
Qualcomm Women InNovemberators in Wireless Scholarship	**March**
Cisco Women Cybersecurity Academy Scholarship	**April**
Accenture Women Cloud Computing Scholarship	**February**
Deloitte Women in Data Science Scholarship	**February**
PwC Women in Analytics Fellowship	**March**
Ernst & Young (EY) Women in STEM Program	**March**

Scholarship	Deadline
KPMG Women in Technology Scholarship	**March**
Bain & Company Women in Tech Scholarship	**March**
McKinsey Women in Data & Digital Fellowship	**March**

International Student Scholarships

Scholarship	Deadline
Fulbright Foreign Student Program	**Varies by country**
Hubert H. Humphrey Fellowship Program	**Varies by country**
Joint Japan/World Bank Graduate Scholarship Program	**February**
Organization of American States Academic Scholarship Program	**Varies by country**
Civil Society Leadership Awards (CSLA)	**Program paused (historically relevant)**
American Association of University Women International Fellowships	**November**
P.E.O. International Peace Scholarship	**December**
Rotary Foundation Global Grants	**Rolling**
Institute of International Education Scholar Rescue Fund	**Rolling**
International Education Financial Aid (IEFA) Scholarships	**Varies**
Aga Khan Foundation International Scholarship Program	**March**
Ford Foundation International Fellowships Program	**Varies by region**
Knight-Hennessy Scholars Program	**October**
Schwarzman Scholars Program	**September**
Yenching Academy of Peking University Scholarship	**December**
Chevening Scholarship Program	**November**
DAAD USA Scholarships	**Varies by scholarship type**
Erasmus Mundus Joint Master Degrees	**December to January**
Gates Cambridge Scholarship	**December**
Rhodes Scholarship	**July to October**
Marshall Scholarship	**September**
Mitchell Scholarship	**September**

Scholarship	Deadline
Churchill Scholarship	**October**
Cambridge Trust International Scholarships	**December**
Oxford University Clarendon Fund Scholarships	**January**
London School of Economics Graduate Support Scheme	**April**
University College London Global Excellence Scholarship	**May**
Imperial College London President's Scholarship	**Varies by intake**
University of Edinburgh Global Scholarship	**April**
University of Glasgow Excellence Scholarship	**Varies by program**
University of Manchester Global Futures Scholarship	**June**
University of Oxford Weidenfeld-Hoffmann Scholarship	**January**
Sciences Po Emile Boutmy Scholarship	**December to February**
Sorbonne University International Merit Scholarship	**April**
ETH Zurich Excellence Scholarship	**December**
EPFL Excellence Fellowships	**April and December**
Swiss Government Excellence Scholarship	**November**
University of Melbourne International Research Scholarship	**Ongoing**
Australian Awards Scholarship Program	**April**
Monash University International Leadership Scholarship	**Varies by round**
University of Sydney International Research Scholarship	**September**
University of Queensland Global Leaders Scholarship	**November for Semester 1, May for Semester 2**
University of Western Australia International Achievement Award	**Varies by intake**
University of Adelaide Global Scholarship	**Varies**
New Zealand International Doctoral Research Scholarships	**July**
New Zealand Development Scholarships	**March**
University of Auckland International Student Excellence Scholarship	**April and November**

Scholarship	Deadline
Victoria University of Wellington International Excellence Scholarship	**June**
University of Otago International Postgraduate Scholarship	**Open year-round**
Canadian Commonwealth Scholarship Program	**March**
Vanier Canada Graduate Scholarships	**November**
Trudeau Foundation Scholarships	**December**
University of Toronto Lester B. Pearson International Scholarships	**January**
University of British Columbia International Leader of Tomorrow Award	**December**
McGill University International Major Entrance Scholarship	**January**
University of Alberta International Student Scholarship	**January**
University of Calgary International Student Award	**December**
York University Global Leader of Tomorrow Award	**February**
Carleton University Prestige Scholarship for International Students	**March**
Dalhousie University International Student Scholarships	**January**
Simon Fraser University International Undergraduate Entrance Scholarship	**March**
Concordia University International Excellence Award	**February**
Laval University International Scholarships	**Varies by program**
Memorial University International Entrance Scholarship	**March**
University of Waterloo International Master's and Doctoral Awards	**Rolling**
University of Manitoba International Undergraduate Scholarship	**October**
University of Saskatchewan International Excellence Award	**February**
Queen's University International Admission Scholarship	**February**
Ryerson University International Student Merit Scholarship	**March**

Scholarship	Deadline
Brock University International Student Scholarship	**April**
University of Ottawa Excellence Scholarship for International Students	**April**
United World Colleges (UWC) Davis Scholars Program	**Varies by institution**
East-West Center Graduate Degree Fellowship	**December**
Asian Development Bank–Japan Scholarship Program	**April**
Korea Foundation for Advanced Studies Scholarship	**September**
Seoul National University Global Scholarship	**March and September**
Yonsei University Underwood International College Scholarship	**March and September**
Korea University Global Leader Scholarship	**March and September**
Chinese Government Scholarship (CSC)	**April**
Tsinghua University Schwarzman Scholars (International Branch)	**September**
Peking University International Scholarship	**April**
Fudan University International Scholarship	**May**
Shanghai Jiao Tong University International Student Scholarship	**March**
Hong Kong PhD Fellowship Scheme	**December**
City University of Hong Kong International Merit Award	**January**
University of Hong Kong International Student Scholarship	**December**
Lingnan University International Scholarship	**March**
Chinese University of Hong Kong Global Leaders Scholarship	**January**
Nanyang Technological University Nanyang Scholarship	**January**
National University of Singapore President's Graduate Fellowship	**January and August**
Singapore Management University International Scholarship	**March**
Singapore University of Technology and Design Global Scholarship	**February**

Scholarship	Deadline
Middle East Studies Association Scholarship Program	**February**
Qatar Foundation International Scholarships	**April**
King Abdullah University of Science and Technology (KAUST) Fellowship	**Rolling**
American University in Cairo Graduate Fellowships	**March**
Al Akhawayn University International Student Scholarship	**June**
African Leadership University Global Scholarship	**Rolling**
Mandela Rhodes Scholarship	**April**
Carnegie Endowment Global Scholars Program	**January**

Graduate & Postgraduate Scholarships

Scholarship	Deadline
Rhodes Scholarship	**Early October**
Marshall Scholarship	**Late September**
Mitchell Scholarship	**Late September**
Gates Cambridge Scholarship	**Varies by citizenship (October or December)**
Churchill Scholarship	**Early November**
Fulbright U.S. Student Program	**Early October**
National Science Foundation Graduate Research Fellowship (NSF GRFP)	**Late October**
Hertz Fellowship	**October**
Department of Defense National Defense Science & Engineering Graduate Fellowship (NDSEG)	**December**
Department of Energy Computational Science Graduate Fellowship (CSGF)	**January**
NIH Oxford-Cambridge Scholars Program	**Early December**
Ford Foundation Predoctoral Fellowship	**December**
Ford Foundation Dissertation Fellowship	**December**
Mellon/ACLS Dissertation Completion Fellowship	**October**
Woodrow Wilson National Fellowship Foundation Graduate Scholarships	**Varies by fellowship track**
Knight-Hennessy Scholars Program (Stanford University)	**Early October**

Scholarship	Deadline
Paul & Daisy Soros Fellowships for New Americans	**October**
Jacob K. Javits Fellowship Program (legacy)	**Legacy program (not currently active)**
Howard Hughes Medical Institute Gilliam Fellowship	**February**
American Association of University Women (AAUW) Fellowships	**November**
National GEM Consortium Fellowship (STEM graduate programs)	**November**
Smith Richardson Foundation Fellowships	**December**
Harry S. Truman Scholarship (graduate funding component)	**Early February**
Thomas R. Pickering Foreign Affairs Fellowship	**September**
Charles B. Rangel Graduate Fellowship	**September**
Donald M. Payne International Development Graduate Fellowship	**November**
Carnegie Endowment Junior Fellows Program	**January**
Scoville Peace Fellowship	**October and January**
Brookings Institution Fellowship Programs	**Varies by program**
Congressional Black Caucus Foundation Fellowships (graduate-level)	**Varies**
Congressional Hispanic Caucus Institute Graduate Fellowships	**December**
Udall Foundation Native American Graduate Fellowship	**March**
Morris K. Udall and Stewart L. Udall Foundation Fellowship Programs	**Varies by track**
Switzer Environmental Fellowship Program	**January**
Swanson Fellowship in Public Service	**March**
Social Science Research Council Graduate Fellowships	**Varies by track**
National Academy of Education Dissertation Fellowship	**October**
Spencer Foundation Dissertation Fellowship	**October**
American Council of Learned Societies Fellowships	**September–November**
American Association for the Advancement of Science (AAAS) Fellowships	**November**

Scholarship	Deadline
American Psychological Association Doctoral Fellowships	**January**
American Sociological Association Minority Fellowship Program	**January**
American Political Science Association Fellowships	**Varies by track**
American Historical Association Graduate Fellowships	**February**
American Anthropological Association Fellowships	**February**
American Economic Association Graduate Fellowships	**January**
American Statistical Association Fellowships	**December**
American Mathematical Society Graduate Fellowships	**February**
American Chemical Society Graduate Fellowship	**October**
American Physical Society Graduate Fellowship	**November**
American Institute of Chemical Engineers Fellowships	**January**
American Society of Civil Engineers Graduate Scholarships	**February**
American Institute of Architects Fellowships	**January**
American Bar Foundation Graduate Fellowship	**December**
American Medical Association Graduate Fellowships	**March**
American Dental Association Foundation Fellowships	**February**
American Nursing Association Doctoral Fellowships	**March**
American Pharmacists Association Foundation Graduate Fellowship	**February**
American Speech-Language-Hearing Association Graduate Fellowships	**May**
American Counseling Association Graduate Fellowships	**March**
American Public Health Association Fellowships	**February**
American Society for Microbiology Fellowships	**January**
American Institute of Biological Sciences Graduate Scholarships	**February**
American Geophysical Union Graduate Research Fellowship	**March**

Scholarship	Deadline
Geological Society of America Graduate Fellowships	**February**
American Meteorological Society Graduate Fellowships	**January**
American Astronomical Society Graduate Fellowships	**January**
American Institute of Physics Graduate Fellowships	**February**
American Mathematical Society Travel & Study Fellowships	**February**
Sigma Xi Scientific Research Society Fellowships	**March and October**
Phi Kappa Phi Graduate Fellowship	**April**
Phi Beta Kappa Graduate Fellowships	**February**
Alpha Kappa Alpha Sorority Graduate Fellowship	**April**
Alpha Phi Alpha Fraternity Graduate Fellowship	**May**
National Black MBA Association Graduate Fellowship	**June**
Prospanica Foundation Graduate Fellowship	**April**
National Association of Black Accountants Graduate Fellowship	**May**
Society of Women Engineers Graduate Fellowship	**February**
Association for Women in Science Graduate Fellowship	**March**
Association for Women in Mathematics Graduate Fellowship	**January**
Association for Women in Psychology Graduate Fellowship	**February**
Point Foundation Graduate Scholarship (LGBTQ, graduate track)	**January**
Soroptimist International Fellowship for Women in Graduate Study	**November**
PEO International Peace Scholarship (graduate women)	**December**
International Women's Forum Graduate Fellowship	**March**
American Association of University Women Selected Professions Fellowship	**December**
Junior League Graduate Fellowship Program	**March**
National Organization for Women Foundation Graduate Fellowship	**April**

Scholarship	Deadline
National Council of Teachers of Mathematics Graduate Fellowships	**May**
Council for Exceptional Children Doctoral Fellowships	**February**
American Educational Research Association Dissertation Fellowship	**November**
Educational Testing Service Graduate Fellowship Program	**December**
International Reading Association Graduate Fellowship	**March**
National Communication Association Doctoral Fellowships	**February**
Modern Language Association Graduate Fellowships	**December**
American Comparative Literature Association Fellowships	**March**
Renaissance Society of America Fellowships (graduate-level)	**December**
Medieval Academy of America Graduate Fellowships	**February**
Folger Shakespeare Library Fellowships	**December**
Dumbarton Oaks Research Library Fellowships	**November**

Community Service & Leadership Scholarships

Scholarship	Deadline
Prudential Emerging Visionaries Scholarship	**November**
Jefferson Awards Students in Action Scholarship	**Varies by local chapter**
Equitable Excellence Scholarship	**December**
Coca-Cola Leaders of Promise Scholarship	**April**
GE-Reagan Foundation Scholarship (leadership focus)	**January**
Elks National Foundation Most Valuable Student Scholarship (leadership branch)	**November**
Burger King Scholars Program (service emphasis)	**December**
Gloria Barron Prize for Young Heroes	**April**
DoSomething.org Easy Scholarships (community projects)	**Varies year-round**
Points of Light Civic Engagement Scholarship	**Rolling nominations**

Scholarship	Deadline
Daily Point of Light Scholarship	**Rolling nominations**
National Caring Awards Youth Scholarship	**March**
Spirit of Service Award Scholarship	**Varies annually**
Bonner Scholars Program	**Set by participating school**
Bonner Leader Program Scholarships	**Varies by campus**
LeaderShape Institute Scholarship	**Varies by institution**
National Student Leadership Conference Scholarships	**Spring, varies**
Hugh O'Brian Youth Leadership (HOBY) Scholarships	**Varies by local chapter**
Rotary Youth Leadership Awards Scholarships	**Varies by Rotary Club**
Lions Club International Youth Leadership Scholarship	**Spring, varies by local club**
Optimist International Leadership Scholarship	**Varies by local Optimist Clubs**
Kiwanis Youth Leadership Scholarship	**March**
Jaycees Youth Leadership Scholarship	**Spring**
Congressional Award Gold Medal Scholarship	**Varies by recognition schedule**
American Legion Auxiliary Girls State Scholarships	**Varies by state program**
American Legion Boys State Scholarships	**Varies by state program**
YMCA Youth & Government Scholarships	**Varies by state**
YWCA Young Women in Leadership Scholarships	**Spring**
Girl Scouts Gold Award Leadership Scholarship	**Varies annually**
Boy Scouts Eagle Scout Leadership Award	**January**
4-H Youth Leadership Awards Scholarship	**Varies by state 4-H office**
FFA Leadership Scholarships	**January**
FCCLA Leadership Scholarships	**March**
BPA Student Leadership Awards	**February**
HOSA Leadership Scholarships	**March**
SkillsUSA Leadership Scholarships	**February**
DECA Emerging Leader Scholarship	**January**
TSA Leadership Scholarship	**March**
Junior Achievement Leadership Scholarship	**March**
National Beta Club Leadership Scholarship	**January**

Scholarship	Deadline
NHS Leadership in Service Award Scholarship	**December**
Phi Theta Kappa Leadership Scholarships	**Varies by institution**
Golden Key International Honour Society Leadership Awards	**June**
Order of the Arrow Leadership Award Scholarships	**February**
Eagle Scout National Leadership Scholarships	**January**
Girl Scouts Juliette Gordon Low Leadership Award	**Varies by council**
Collegiate Leadership Competition Scholarships	**Spring**
National Society of High School Scholars Leadership Awards	**Varies annually**
National Society of Leadership and Success Scholarships	**Varies annually**
Sigma Alpha Pi National Leadership Scholarships	**Fall and Spring cycles**
Alpha Phi Omega Service & Leadership Scholarships	**March**
Alpha Kappa Delta Phi Leadership Scholarships	**Spring**
Alpha Phi Alpha Leadership Awards	**Varies annually**
Alpha Kappa Alpha Leadership Awards	**February**
Kappa Alpha Psi Leadership Scholarships	**Varies annually**
Omega Psi Phi Leadership Awards	**Spring**
Delta Sigma Theta Leadership Scholarships	**Varies annually**
Kappa Alpha Psi Leadership Scholarships	**Varies annually**
Sigma Lambda Beta Leadership Scholarships	**Spring**
Sigma Lambda Gamma Leadership Scholarships	**Spring**
National Black MBA Association Leadership Scholarship	**Spring**
Prospanica Leadership Scholarships	**Spring**
SHPE Community Leadership Scholarships	**Spring**
NSBE Leadership Development Scholarship	**Spring**
AISES Leadership in STEM Scholarship	**Spring**
American Red Cross Youth Leadership Scholarship	**Spring**
Habitat for Humanity Youth Leadership Scholarship	**Spring**
United Way Youth Leadership Awards	**Spring**
Salvation Army Leadership Scholarships	**Spring**
Junior League Community Service Scholarship	**Spring**
National Charity League Scholarships	**Spring**
Jack Kent Cooke Foundation Young Leaders Scholarship	**November**

Scholarship	Deadline
Ron Brown Scholar Program (leadership track)	**January**
Davidson Fellows Leadership Scholarship	**February**
Cameron Impact Scholarship (leadership emphasis)	**September**
Milken Scholars Program (service & leadership emphasis)	**December**
Posse Foundation Leadership Scholarship	**Varies by city**
QuestBridge College Prep Leadership Awards	**March**
QuestBridge National Leadership Scholarship	**September**
Dell Scholars Program Leadership Award	**December**
Greenhouse Scholars Leadership Award	**December**
Coca-Cola Community College Academic Team Scholarship	**December**
Phi Beta Kappa Key into Public Service Scholarship	**January**
Public Service Fellows Program (various universities)	**Varies by institution**
Center for Public Integrity Leadership Fellowship	**Spring**
Truman Scholarship (public service leadership)	**February**
Udall Scholarship (leadership in environment & policy)	**March**
Hollings Scholarship (NOAA leadership in environment)	**January**
Public Policy & International Affairs (PPIA) Fellowship (leadership track)	**November**
Coro Fellows Program in Public Affairs	**January**
New Leaders Council Fellowship	**November**
Humanity in Action Fellowship	**January**
Emerging Leaders in Energy Scholarship	**Spring**
Young Leaders in Social Entrepreneurship Scholarship	**Spring**